Contents

Introduction

"They think it's such a little thing. Why worry when they say 'God came to save all *men* ?' They say it doesn't matter. It does matter! You are saying it does not matter what I feel. And I feel excluded!"

— *Woman in New Guinea*

"I began to feel for her the hurt she experienced. And I just made my mind up that I was going to do something to bring about an alleviation of this."

— *Msgr. Thoralf (Korby) Thielen*
1921-1993

Their voices ringing with laughter, pain, and frustration, over three hundred Catholic women in nine countries of Africa and southern Asia embraced two profound questions with a rare sense of freedom: "As a woman in the Catholic Church, are you able to live your Christian life to the fullest? Does the Catholic Church address women's equality in your culture?"

The late Msgr. Thoralf (Korby) Thielen, of the Josephinum Seminary in Columbus, Ohio, posed these questions to small gatherings of women from South Africa to India to New Guinea. Thielen had dedicated his retirement to the cause of Christian treatment for women of the world, and began his quest by recording the stories they told him in church basements, living rooms, huts, or wherever they best could gather. This book is a compilation of these women's voices.

To be sure, no one single story prevails. For some women, respect and dignity means recognition of the roles that women play in scripture and in the history of the Church. Others seek greater respect for the ministry of women in today's Catholic Church, for the women who teach and heal and carry communion to villages in the back country. Some envision wider roles for women in tomorrow's Church. Others simply need the Church to speak out for them today, to address the wider cultural traditions and say unequivocally that oppressive treatment of women is morally wrong. Too often they find silence instead.

They are women berated and beaten by husbands married more to tradition than to wives. Humiliated by Churchmen who dismiss their pleas. Strengthened by their own achievements as pastoral ministers, religious education directors, and social reformers. From New Guinea to Uganda to India to South Africa, the women Fr. Korby chatted with are a diverse lot. Some of the speakers are highly educated sisters, and some are poor village housewives. They are grandmothers, wives, and young high school women.

These women speak in a medley of voices; yet it is no great stretch to say that the woman from Kenya speaks a nearly universal tongue when she tells Korby, "There are many of us who have highly-developed gifts, and we aren't able to use them in the context of the Church." And Fr. Korby answers them, "I'll tell you what I think about equality. Jesus said that he came so we could have life, and have it to the full. And that's for every man and woman to have full life."

For Fr. Korby, life was as rich as the deep, dark earth of home. Born on May 23, 1921, on a farm in Dubuque County, Iowa, Thoralf Thielen was known more affectionately to his family and friends as "Bud," later as Father Bud. But, as his seminary friend and spiritual soul-mate Msgr. David Gernatt puts it, he was too big and full of life to be known by just one nickname. With three other "Bud"s at seminary, he became Korby, the name by which he was known to friends across the United States and indeed throughout the world.

Korby came to the Josephinum Seminary in September 1935 for his high school, college, and seminary training, and was ordained in 1947. Following his ordination, he studied for three years at the Pontifical Gregorian University in Rome and at the University of Fribourg in Switzerland, earning S.T.L. and S.T.D. degrees. He was a professor of Theology at the Josephinum from 1950-1961, and served as Dean of the Theological School from 1967-1971. Later he was Director of Theological Field Education and taught Counseling and Communications at the Josephinum until his retirement in 1986.

Fr. Korby's varied interests and commitments deeply enriched his life. Despite his busy schedule, Korby took up flying, and his love of the skies led him to become Chaplain first in the Ohio National Guard and then in the U.S. Air Force. Indeed, his Air Force travels were his first link to establishing friendships throughout the world. Fr. Korby was a leading expert in the ecumenical movement as well. His publications include *What Is an Ecumenical Council?*, a work for which he received special commendation from Pope John XXIII. Another interest of his was National Marriage Encounter. He served as National Chaplain from 1979-1982, and continued his involvement beyond his retirement. In a homily to Marriage Encounter couples in Uganda in 1991, Korby said, "To communicate, people must have listening as their top priority — real communication requires LISTENING, real drinking in the meaning of what the other person says."

The art of listening, real listening, and his role as a marriage counselor attuned Fr. Korby to the problems faced by women in the broader culture. But it was at the Josephinum that he began to think of women's equality in the context of the Catholic Church. For all his pleasant memories of his teaching days, he observed that many of the male faculty — particularly those who hailed from foreign nations — looked down upon a fine, caring, and competent female colleague with whom Korby worked closely. His work and conversations with Ladora (not her real name), attuned Fr. Korby to the need for equality in the Catholic Church. Furthermore, he observed qualities in Ladora that he and other men generally lacked, and was convinced that the Church would benefit by opening up to women's gifts. Indeed, the Church needed to become an advocate for women. Korby maintained that Jesus had promoted respect for women in his own day, in a culture that was even more patriarchal than our own.

At the same time, Fr. Korby was hearing from some Churchmen that equality issues only concerned women in the United States and a handful of other western countries. This line of thinking held that equality was not a concern of women in other parts of the world. Korby's extensive travels for work and vacations convinced him that this was not true. He knew that Catholic women throughout the world craved equality, and he made it his retirement goal to record their voices saying so.

In September 1991, Fr. Korby and Fr. Dave Gernatt — Korby's friend of fifty-six years — embarked on a fifty-four day tour to listen to women across the world. The first recorded conversations took place at Fr. Dave's home parish in West Seneca, New York. The next stop was London, England. But the remainder of the tour took the priests to the women of Africa and southern Asia. In fifty-four days, Fr. Korby and Fr. Dave spoke with over thirty groups of women in Kenya, Uganda, Malawi, South Africa, India, Sri Lanka, Thailand, The Philippines, and New Guinea.

Priests, sisters, and lay persons whom Korby had befriended in earlier travels welcomed them with open arms and helped with arrangements. Korby's cheerful, hearty demeanor and boisterous laugh endeared him to ordinary folk and helped break down communication barriers. Fr. Dave tells a story of Korby lavishing hearty praise on a woman who had gone out of her way to prepare a special dinner — fried chicken that could hardly be chewed — for Korby and Dave. Korby's appreciation for her efforts bridged the woman's meager knowledge of English. "Boy, that's good!" he boomed in that voice of his that fills a kitchen. Later, Fr. Dave kidded Korby: "Was saying 'Yummy' a lie?" "No," Korby said, "I was being kind — trying to make her feel good."

His kind and open nature encouraged women to speak of things about which they would normally keep silent. Some spoke to him at great risk. If the wrong ears heard them, or even heard that they had come to speak, they might be beaten by husbands or sanctioned in their jobs. While Fr. Korby hoped to compile the conversations into a book as a means of shedding light on the issue of women's equality, he would also need to protect the women's identities. The speakers would have to be presented anonymously, referred to as "a woman in Kenya," "a woman in New Guinea," etc. It was more important to let their voices be heard, and let it be known that these voices rang out across the world.

A life-long priest and theologian, Korby didn't set out to embarrass the Catholic Church. Rather, he wanted to provide a wake-up call that some of its members were hurting. Of course, many changes were already occurring and have occurred since Korby's trip in 1991. New roles have opened up for women, and the Church has begun to recognize the historical shortcomings in its treatment of women. Still, many issues and controversies remain. As to the possibility that his work might yet raise a few eyebrows, Korby laughed and said, "I've spent my whole life swimming upstream!"

Upstream held a bigger obstacle, however. Fr. Korby had conceived of his tour on a Medjugorie pilgrimage in thanksgiving for his successful battle with thyroid cancer. But after the ten-nation tour was completed, and just as the long work of transcribing the tapes was about to get underway, Korby was afflicted with a fast-growing lung cancer. In the early fall of 1993, Korby learned that he had only a short time to live. Among his many preparations for death and good-byes, his project weighed heavily on his mind. Fr. Dave explains how Korby wished to have this project seen through to completion:

> In late October, 1993, I received a phone call from his family telling me that the Mayo Clinic predicted he had only a couple of weeks to live. I called my dearest friend immediately and said, "I'm coming out to see you." "When?" he said. I said, "Within two days I'll be on my way." His reply was, "Why don't you wait until I get home?" "I want to see you while you are still lucid," I responded. His retort was, "When did that happen?"
>
> My housekeeper, Mary Jane Casey, and I stayed in his home to help his family take care of him in his last days on

earth. On Wednesday, November 3 (1993), he put his head down on the kitchen table and said, "Dave, I think I have only three or four more days to live." I stared at my dearest friend as reality set in. He raised up again and shaking his head, said, "But, oh Dave, the book! I wanted that work completed before I went." I assured him that I would do what I could to bring his project to fruition. I was deeply touched when a priest friend visited him and Father Korby said, "Dave knows my heart."

Msgr. Thielen died on November 6, 1993. A week before his death he had given his final homily in a communal Sacrament of the Anointing of the Sick. There he expressed his vision of the grandeur of death, of life with God:

> So I am looking forward to an explosion into the universe. Because here — well, really, I'm getting out of prison. To be leaving the prison of this body and joining with Jesus and the Lord — to be able to expand into the universe.

Fr. Korby's project broadened into a wider family endeavor after his death. Korby was my mother's cousin, and as a child I delighted in his once or twice-a-year drop-in visits. His hearty laugh, his sincere concern for the pains and aches and slippages of family members who were growing older, and his celebration of births and weddings resounded through our kitchen. When I learned that Fr. Dave needed someone to carry on Korby's project, I jumped at the chance. My wife and I — as well as my colleagues at Loras College — were very much concerned about the equality of women in the Church and beyond. Furthermore, the project would be a memorial to Fr. Korby and to my mother, now deceased.

The family connection grew. The project would have gone nowhere without my niece Sherri Koch, who painstakingly transcribed over 20 tapes, long hours spent deciphering thick accents through buzzing tape recorder noise. My mother-in-law, Rosemary Noonan, also transcribed one of the tapes (and a few more were transcribed by Loras College student Adriana Beltran, from Colombia.) My wife Dianne has been an ongoing source of help and feedback as I excerpted from the transcripts and arranged and organized the material.

Other words of acknowledgment are in order as well. Fr. Dave Gernatt has been unfailing in his pledge to see Korby's project carried through. His friend, Mary Jane Casey, has helped, too, to fill me in on details of Korby's thinking. Finally, the many relatives of Fr. Korby in and around his and my home in Dubuque, Iowa, have supported this project wholeheartedly.

The greatest appreciation, however, must be extended to the women of Africa, southern Asia, London, and West Seneca, New York, who opened their hearts to Fr. Korby and shared their hopes and frustrations. And to Fr. Korby, who envisioned better lives for women throughout the world.

What you will encounter here is a compilation of the voices from Fr. Korby's conversations. It is not a work of theology, nor is there any attempt to analyze or critique the responses. These are, instead, the voices themselves, a sampling of what Catholic women across the world *are saying* about their desire to *RISE WITH CHRIST.*

— Kevin Koch, Ph.D.
Loras College, Dubuque, Iowa

Postscript: A dramatized reading of portions of these conversations is available through Msgr. David Gernatt, 11742 Markham Road, Gowanda, NY 14070. The reading was given at Loras College, Dubuque, IA, on March 20, 1996, as part of Women's History Month.

Rev. Msgr. Thoralf T. Thielen
May 23, 1921 - November 6, 1993

Preface
Storying

NEW GUINEA

Korby   We found that the most effective way to transform people spiritually is to get them to tell their own faith story in small groups. Because everybody has a story to tell.

Woman   I think that would fit so well with our people because they are naturally born story-tellers. Their life centers around telling stories. You know, if you're talking to somebody and one of the nationals comes along and says, "Oh, what are you doing?", we say, "We're storying." Not, "We're having a chat." "We're storying."

Korby   Sure. Well, that's the old, old way that the scripture stories were handed on before they were written down.

Woman   Yeah. Jesus told stories.

Chapter One

Women in Scripture

The women Korby speaks with reflect on the role of Mary Magdalene and other women of scripture and the early Church. Over time, cultural restrictions against women won out over Jesus' liberating message. But Jesus himself was counter-cultural and treated women with the dignity and respect that ancient society refused. Perhaps this is even a sign of Christ's divinity. The Church today, the women agree, needs to be like Jesus and respect women, even when that runs counter to local culture and tradition. The Church needs to break through cultural taboos.

Saint Paul presents a surface stumbling block to women's equality when his dictum, "Wives, obey your husbands," is taken out of context. A marriage relationship should involve a mutual atmosphere of respect and love. Often, the counter-charge for husbands to love their wives is forgotten, not preached, or not heard.

KENYA

Korby   How do you feel about Christ? Did he treat women and men equally, or did he want to and wasn't able to, or what?

Woman   When you look at the Gospels, we find great hope. We find that the way Jesus treated the women was counter-cultural. For example, you know, if a woman had committed adultery, according to the

Jewish law, she was supposed to be killed. OK, but Jesus kind of says, OK.

Korby   OK, don't do it again.

Woman   Don't do it again. But actually he makes this woman realize that she *is* something. I'm sure that she never knew that she was anything. But this man here makes her feel that she is somebody.

Korby   She is somebody. Right. He went counter-cultural there. He cut through taboos. Sure. And sending Mary Magdalene to the apostles.

Woman   I know. And Jesus, the way he talks to her, deep theology. And even revealed himself to her in the Resurrection.

Korby   Yeah. Yeah, I've heard it said that the way we see him treating women is really another sign of his divinity. Because he could not have done it and gotten away with it if he hadn't been divine.

Woman   Yeah. Because actually that would perplex the people. But like, for example, that woman at the well. The apostles gasped. What has happened?

Korby   Yeah, right. You just don't do that.

Woman   But no one took him to court! See, all of these things, I think, for me I feel that the Church should be like that. That's what the Church should be in any culture. The Church, like Christ, should be counter-cultural. So that it is not just part of the get-corrupted, get-aligned social reality. And the human reality is female and male together. But our Church has not done that.

SRI LANKA

Woman Christ treated everybody the same, both men and women. He never treated the women badly, just because they are women. Say like with Mary Magdalene, he didn't reject her like men did. He helped her, he listened to her. With the other women, too. Even women that men considered bad or impure because of the culture. Those that were different he helped. They all were treated the same, equally.

Korby What he did was to break through a lot of the Jewish taboos and the traditions. I guess that's the example he gives us. We have to break through a lot of taboos.

Woman It takes a lot of courage to break through bad customs, to break customs in order to give freedom to the ladies. But Jesus had to have courage.

Korby Right. You just gave me another idea. What we need more of, I guess, is priests who have the courage to break through the customs and the taboos as Jesus did.

SRI LANKA

Korby Do you think that the Church has been trying to do anything effectively to conquer inequality?

Woman No, I don't. Because even still today they say that the husband should always be respected. They still say, "Obedience to the husband!" You have to do whatever he asks you to do. That is what the Church is teaching. In the homes, the mothers teach their daughters the same, "Women have to respect their husband above all." That is why the women are oppressed; they can't expect nothing else.

Korby I wonder what you think of the interpretation of that passage of Saint Paul. Why women should be submissive to their husbands. Is there another part to that teaching? Do you understand what I am saying? The teaching you expressed comes mainly from Saint Paul to the Ephesians, Chapter 5. But there is another part, the next paragraph. "Husbands must love their wives as Christ loved the Church." That part the Church doesn't teach?

Woman No. (Other women laugh.)

Korby I kind of thought Saint Paul meant that the proper relationship between husband and wife was that you must keep this part of the bargain, and you must keep this part. So what you are saying is that the Church has been emphasizing the idea of obedience and service and so on, without underlying the idea of love?

Woman Yes, I think most places only teach the first part. The husbands don't listen to the duties of the husband. You see, the husband sometimes thinks what he wants. He feels as if, "I am master. I am the boss!" This is the mentality from the beginning. It is the culture.

Korby The Church has not done much to go against the culture?

Woman The thing is, it's an accepted law here. The majority accept this. There are a few individuals who are working to bring this liberation, but the Church as a whole is not doing it.

KENYA

Korby   Do you think that Christ treated men and women with equal respect?

[An interpreter speaks for the interviewee.]

Interpreter   She said yes, Jesus was for the equality of men and women. She gave the example of the woman at the well. Jesus did not just speak to men. He took the time to speak to her. He even broke the Jewish law to speak to her. And then there's the example of the resurrection. He did not look for the men; he saw the women first. She said if you look at the Epistles, you see that there were women leaders in the early Church.

Korby   Lydia, Priscilla.

Woman   Yes.

Korby   What do you think about the way Saint Paul spoke about women at different times? What was his thinking?

Interpreter   It says to obey, but you have to look very carefully. Now she has dropped the word "obey" and has adopted another word, "respect." She made a very interesting change there. Not talking about obeying, she is talking about respect.

Korby   As I am picking it up, you do what your husband wants if it is respecting your person.

Interpreter   I asked her if he sent her out to steal, would she go? She said no, I would not. I would explain to him that respect is found in the truth.

Korby I always thought that the relationship there Saint Paul was talking about was, yes, wives should respect their husbands. But the husband must love his wife.

Interpreter But at first hearing it sounds. . .

Korby   It sounds like a put-down.

KENYA

Woman   We cannot decide to change the culture of the Bible. Because in that way we make a very big mistake. In the beginning, Adam was created. The woman was not created from earth, you see, like Adam. But he took to sleep. . . .

Korby   Yeah, sleep.

Woman   And then God made the woman out of that man. It's like a weak place of a man. She is someone to be coddled by a man always. So we naturally think we are the weaker sex on the side of the spiritual. We cannot mix the spiritual side of it with our own culture and civilization. Because that would sort of take the place of God. Our own interests, our needs, would come and take the place of God.

Korby   OK, that is certainly wonderful. Where does culture fit in? Culture influences the Church. And we need to ask, then, what about the culture that expressed the ideas which are in scripture? In speaking to Jewish rabbis, they say that the real concept there is that man and woman are two parts of one whole. That the rib is understood as being part of a whole. Man and a woman together are one. And that it's not a part of weakness, or something like that.

> That's what I think. But I'm getting in here! I'm supposed to be listening, see!

Woman Yes, Father. I think this equality thing is not as simple as this to discuss.

INDIA

Woman 1 Jesus said that God had sent him as his ambassador to the world. Then he said I am sending to you apostles as ambassadors to the world. It was his divine command to all the men and women without exception.

Korby What would you say to, see now I am going to be the devil's advocate, what would you say if someone said, "But he was talking just to the men"?

Woman 1 Just to them?

Korby Just to the men. He was talking just to the apostles.

Woman 2 At that time there were no women apostles. Only men were there.

Woman 1 No, no. Apostles represent the whole world. That remains so, all men and women is understood.

Korby Good. I agree with you. I was just, I say, just playing the devil's advocate there. To understand a little bit more. And what I like to think of, too, is that, you know, the one whom our Lord sent first after the Resurrection, even to tell the apostles, was Mary Magdalene. And even the word "apostle" means somebody with a mission. Somebody to go do something. So he sent her to tell the others. She was really the first apostle. She was the apostle to the apostles.

ENGLAND

Korby   Does anybody have any ideas about the theological or the scriptural underpinnings for the, well, positions, the thoughts, that have been expressed here this afternoon? Is there, can you think of something specifically that you see in scripture that shows that women ought to be treated the same as men?

Woman 1   The resurrection itself because women were the first witnesses. The women were the first at the tomb, to discover that the tomb was empty. And Christ came first to the women.

Korby   Mary Magdalene was the first apostle in that sense, really. Yeah.

Woman 1   Martha and Mary. Mary made the same proclamation of faith as Peter did. And still because she was a woman it wasn't important.

Woman 2   Some thinkers seem to consider that versions of the Gospel were chosen which favored a male-dominated sense, you know, while other writings which were not chosen, didn't.

NEW GUINEA

Woman   Well, I think personally, um, the one guiding thing in my life is from John 10:10, where Christ says, "I have come that you may have life. Life to the fullest."

Korby   I love that.

Woman   And I think the Church is the biggest block to that.

❖   ❖   ❖

KENYA

Woman 1   In the Church, this thing of a woman being inferior, I think this is due to the discussion of the Bible. Right from the beginning, you know the Bible is written by men. And these men are men of the culture.

Korby   Are men of their culture?

Woman 1   Yeah. Look at the Bible. It says that women should always obey men. Women should not talk in front of men. I don't know where that is said in the Bible.

Woman 2   It is in Corinthians. Women should keep quiet.

Woman 1   Yeah, that's what they say. The women should keep quiet. Was it because of the culture of the Corinthians? But why should *we* adopt the culture of the Corinthians? We are Kenyan. Why should we adopt the culture of the Corinthians?

Korby   The Corinthians are dead.

Woman 1   We are alive.

Narrative One
Eucharistic Minister

NEW GUINEA

Woman   Another thing that really got me was when the Pope came to visit, we were going to have a Mass there, an outdoor Mass. And, um, each of the highlands groups, the parishes, all the parishes all over the highlands were to send so many of their catechists, people, to be Eucharistic ministers. So this area, which is a very male-oriented area — that's where the women had to crawl into church to keep their heads lower than the men's — now they're to the stage where they've got women catechists, which is really something. And the women were chosen by the community.

Anyway, this one young girl would have been about twenty-two years old, I guess. She was from this one particular area where they had two men and two women chosen to come be the Communion ministers. Well, she was just thrilled, absolutely thrilled, you know. And when the time came for them to come, they submitted the names. The bishop submitted the names. And these two women who were on . . .

Korby   Got crossed off?

Woman   Word was sent back saying that women were not allowed to do this. She was just so . . .

Korby   Why, devastated.

Woman   It was just like her life.

Korby   That hurts.

Woman   And I thought to myself, I wish, I wish that those fellows would have come over and followed her into the bush. I saw her one Sunday afternoon when she came back. She had come through the bush to give Communion to elderly people who couldn't come to Mass on Sunday. And she would sit down and spend an hour with them, went to each house, and prayed with that person. She had gone through special training with the Bishop. She had, you know, her candle there, and she read something from the scripture in their own language.

And she came back and she was mud to here. Absolute. You see, it had rained and she had to walk through the swamp.

And I wished they have followed her one day.

Korby   Right.

Woman   So there were 250 men who were Eucharistic ministers that day.

Chapter Two

The Church and
the Cultural Tradition

Domestic Violence and Inequality

In the home, women are expected by their culture and traditions to be submissive to their husbands, even to the point of accepting physical abuse. Women are recognized as women only by their ability to bear and raise children. In some locations, even their children do not belong to them; the children belong, instead, to the husband and the husband's clan. Should there be a divorce, the mother will lose her children. Naturally, she endures much for their sake.

The women believe that the Church has largely abdicated its responsibility to address such matters. The Church has maintained that these are local traditions, manifestations of the culture. But Fr. Korby reiterates that Jesus was "counter-cultural" and broke a lot of taboos in Jerusalem.

KENYA

Woman The village that she was married in, she wasn't liked there because if her husband came home drunk and beat her, she would beat him back. So she began to see the importance of standing for what was important to her.

Even her father did not see these beatings as unusual. He saw this as something to expect.

Korby   Abuse of the wife, you mean?

Woman   Yes. A woman's job is to respect her husband. Her
             father said that.

Korby   So this idea of going forward to a greater freedom or
             to a greater equality, that was really generated from
             inside herself rather than with any assistance, let's
             say, from the Church, from the pastor, from the
             priest.

New Guinea

Korby   In the villages, by and large, how do the men treat
             their wives? Is there really, you know, respect and
             dignity? Or do they expect, you know, you do this,
             you do that? Is there a basis of equality?

Woman   No, I don't think so. If you go to the village now,
             you'll see a woman with a great load on her, the
             child on top here, another child here, another here.
             And what is the man carrying? He's carrying his
             knife or his stick, and that's all. And then she has to
             work seven, six days a week. He does two or three.

Korby   What does he do the rest of the time?

Woman   Sit around waiting for his food.

Korby   No wonder the girls want to get out of the village
             into the city, huh?

Woman   If they have a chance to go someplace, they go.

Korby   Yeah.

Woman	Yeah. But then that some other place is no different from their own.

UGANDA

Woman	The children don't even belong to us when we are married. They belong to the clan of the man that we married.
Korby	Oh, boy! And is that still the way it . . .
Woman	That is still the pattern. And even if there is a separation the children don't belong to her.

As for the boy, he is the one who perhaps will enrich the clan by providing more and more people. And if the woman he marries happens to have no children, that woman is going to suffer untold sufferings, and she usually suffers in silence.

SOUTH AFRICA

Korby	Women who decide to become nuns, they give up that ability to become a mother, and that is very difficult. What do you think about the big sacrifice you made, Sister, not to be married or have children?
Woman	It was difficult, because at first my parents did not allow me to become a sister. They think that they need the dowry to get by. But then later on they accepted it. But at first they wouldn't because it's something new in the family. They are not used to a woman or a girl like myself saying they want to be a sister and not get married. Because in Africa if a woman doesn't bear children then she is not re-

garded as a woman. Most of the divorces around the country are caused by that.

Korby   That's interesting. So it is really a counter-cultural action on the part of an African girl to become a sister?

Woman   Yes, most people are surprised because they cannot believe that a woman can learn to live alone without a man around them.

SOUTH AFRICA (HIGH SCHOOL)

Korby   Does it happen that the men will marry, or be living at different times with two, three, or more women?

*Young
Woman 1*   Yes.

*Young   Are men allowed in the Church to be married to
Woman 2*   more than one?

Korby   Is it allowed? Not to be married to more than one, no.

Fr. Dave   It is illegal in the Church, and it's probably illegal in the laws, but would a woman come off and try to prosecute that law? Would she? It's not legal to have two wives in South Africa, right? But now, you are the first wife, will you go to the police and tell that your husband has two wives?

*Young   NO! I can't!
Woman 2*

Korby   Why not?

Young Woman 2	Because it is their decision, and no one can say anything. The laws have changed. But the people running the shops, do they listen to the laws? The policeman, does he listen?

UGANDA

Man	At the very beginning, getting married, making the vows in front of the priest, I say to her that "I love you." I don't say, "I respect you." There is something missing somewhere.
Korby	That should be in there.

SOUTH AFRICA

Woman 1	I said to a teacher, "Why do you think God created women?" and he said, "To wait on the men." And I said, "Where do you get that idea?" And he said, "It's in the Bible." And I said, "You bring me the text and I'll give you ten grand!" And I'm still....
Korby	And you still have the ten grand!
Woman 1	Yes!
Korby	Where do you think young boys get those ideas? From their mothers or fathers?
Woman 2	It's our culture.
Woman 1	It's a tradition of ours. Men are superior, as head of the family.

Korby   So the man in the family would give his boys that idea, or does the mother help to give that idea?

Woman 2   The father, the grandsons, it is definitely passed on.

Woman 3   A lot of this is your fault because you put yourself
(Older   in the position of accepting it. But you don't accept
Woman)   everything from the culture. Your clothes are different from what your grandmother wore.

Woman 1   No, but we must obey the regulations.

Korby   Should these traditions be changed?

Woman 2   I don't think it should be changed because it is something we deserved from our grandmother and grandfather.

Korby   So are you saying that you like it that way?

Woman 2   Oh, yes!

Woman 3   You *like* to be in an inferior position?

Woman 2   Because like in the family, when some problem arises, I can't be able to solve the problem. I must take it to the man.

Woman 3   Why? God gave *you* a brain!

Woman 2   For the man to solve the problems.

Woman 3   Why? Your brains are not the same? Is his brain superior to yours?

Woman 2   No. But Adam was the first person made by God. We are not meant for the same . . .

Woman 3   Do you mean because of chronological. . . .?

Woman 2   I am a married woman. T and I have been married fifteen years. We have a relationship — that is, I consider myself to be equal with T. And we see that we have different roles in our marriage. And we can mix our roles, or change our roles, but we both bring something different to our marriage. But at the same time, if we have a decision, we both will discuss it. But I believe that God has given T the headship in our family. And if it comes to a decision, an important decision, I will then submit to what T's decision is. But some men abuse the headship thing. And they run the wives and kids from a point of view that "I am in charge and I am in control and I can say whatever I prefer."

Korby   Do you know other people who believe as you do?

Woman 2   Yes. A lot of other people.

Korby   Because there are a lot of African women whom we have spoken to who recognize that this comes from their culture, but they don't like it. Period!

Women   That's us! Yes. Yes.

Woman 2   The girls that I teach have a lot of pride in the fact that they do the traditional women's work. Many of them are bragging to me that when they get home, they were going to do the cooking for the family, and the cleaning. It is a real source of pride to them. That's giving them a sense of worth. This is where they really smile, talk about what they are going to do, to clean and to take care of the children. It is not seen as inferior. This is my role, and I have done it well.

NEW GUINEA

Woman   In my school days, I didn't have trouble with boys because I found that a lot of girls tend to shout back at the boys because they shout something to them. I go straight to them and I tell, you know, what you did was not good. I don't like what you did. And in that way I gained their respect.

Korby   Yeah.

Woman   So I don't believe in shouting at each other, or raising voices high, or things like that. I would say that if we walk along it's side by side. Not that the men will never say "Oh, I go first and you come after me." Of course, I will try to fight him. But not fist fights or things like that. But there are other ways of tackling equality.

Korby   It would be nice if everybody did that.

Woman   I mean, I look back to my grandparents. Traditionally they had, back in the villages, the husband and wife. They don't fight, they don't argue. She knows her job, he knows his job, and they live faithfully until whatever, when one goes. Yeah. And nowadays everybody is fighting. "I want this. I want that." Nobody is saying, "OK, what do you want?" The man doesn't say, "OK, I'll sit down and I'll listen to you." Or the woman doesn't say, "I will listen to you." And if everybody is shouting, nobody is listening.

Korby   If people love one another, they're going to listen. And if they listen, really listen, to what the other's needs and wants are, they will try to respond to it, and you have equality. I suppose maybe we need to emphasize love, love, the love of Christ, and that we're really not loving unless we listen.

SRI LANKA

Woman   The girls come to a certain age, like eighteen. They have finished their school. If you can get a job for them, nowadays the job begins in garment factories. Then they are to find a place to stay. So now we have time to see what we can do for these young girls. We find that is more important even than looking after little children. Because if these big ones are educated properly, then we are building up families. If we can get a piece of land, we can put up a house and tell her this is yours. This is yours.

See, in those days we wouldn't think of that. We thought, all right, if you find a young man, you'll get married and off you go. Finished. But then we are not giving them that leadership. We are not using what they have. Give them a bit of land, give them a little bit of house. And from there you go to work. And you work on your own. And get married to somebody, settle down. You are somebody. So all their qualities, some or other, they will be brought to the forefront.

PHILIPPINES

Woman   With the younger generation, women are asking for equality. When I got married thirty-four years ago, women were supposed to be submissive. But now, when it comes to decision-making in the home, we discuss it, so there is equality in our house. When it comes to education, when it comes to bringing up

our children, there is an equal right between husband and wife, at least in our family.

Korby   Yeah. There seems to be, from what I have heard
from talking with several different groups of women
here in Manila, there's a lot more equality than in
other countries that I've been in. But they are aware
and really working at it. There's unions, groups, that
are making other women aware of it.

Woman   Still, the dumb thing is that once she has a family,
she has to stay and mind the children. It is seen by
society that she has to stay home and a lot of her
education goes down the toilet. Ten, twelve, fifteen
years later when the children are in school and for
her to get back into the work force, she's lost a lot.

INDIA

Woman   We ladies see that we should not break the family.
We see that if we suffer, well, we don't feel like
breaking the family because then the children, they
suffer. And, uh, if they leave their husband, well,
where are they going to stay? If he beats you, if he
hits everything, then also he will give you something
to eat.

SOUTH AFRICA (HIGH SCHOOL)

Young   In our culture, women from childhood are inferior.
Woman   Women are tortured, we must never argue.

Korby   The woman is just really the servant who has to do
the man's bidding?

| Young Woman | Women have to listen to their husband. You just keep quiet and the beating continues. |

SRI LANKA

| Korby | You mentioned beating. Is there a lot of wife beating? |

| Woman | There is, very bad, especially in poor areas. Sometimes the whole night the wife is outside, or on the streets hiding somewhere. They cannot be in the house because the man is drunk. |

| Korby | Does the husband abuse the children also? |

| Woman | Children too. The sisters are keeping children. They come, "Can I stay here with you because Mom is going to work, and the whole night my dad is beating me because he is drunk." |

| Korby | Does the wife sometimes take the abuse in order to protect the children? |

| Woman | Yes, yes, they do. |

| Korby | A lot of it comes out of culture, doesn't it? It's been traditionally that way. |

| Woman | Traditionally, yes. |

| Korby | The Church has not done much to go against the culture. There was a monastery where we were staying where people just come for help. And there was this lady, one morning she needed money to get back home to her parents because that night her husband had threatened to kill her with a crowbar. |

And she wanted to get back to her parents. So the abbot gave her some money because he said what we have to do is stay out of this and let her go back to the parents and let the two families settle it, because if we get into this we can really get into trouble.

But as you know, Christ challenged or broke taboos in Jerusalem.

NEW GUINEA

Woman   What the heck is equality? What is it? In my book it just means a respect for an individual human being. First of all, respect for myself, and acceptance of my talents and my limitations. But it means a respect that you offer to another human being simply because they are human beings.

Korby   Right.

Woman   Not on the basis of their gender, or their education, or their heart, or anything like that. And until we can offer that to each other, we're always going to be in a struggle. And I think there are things built into the structure of society — there are rules, there are customs, there are traditions — which prevent me from respecting myself adequately.

Korby   The Church hasn't done much about countering that.

Woman   No, no.

SOUTH AFRICA

Woman 1   The Christian Family Movement [C.F.M.] is the nucleus of the married couples. We are ready to spread this movement right here from the center, throughout small parishes, in all the small communities.

Korby   Do some of you belong to it? That is working to try to get men and women to really work together. I was with a family in Malaga yesterday. They have much the same problems there as here. The C.F.M. works so that the family we were with, the husband and wife really work together. The husband helped . . . Father Dave and I had dinner with them. Had a meal with them yesterday evening. The husband helped cook the meal . . . .

Woman 2   That doesn't work here. Here you are working and the man is also working, and when you come home from work the husband wants you to do everything.

Korby   Well, see, that's what the Christian Family Movement does. It would help to get husbands to work together with their wives, and not to expect the wives to do everything, when each is working outside.

NEW GUINEA

Woman   You know what makes me proud as a Catholic? What makes me proud is when I see the schools, the hospital, the training college, started by Catholics, and Catholic charity. What a lot of us see is the production of what the Catholic Church has put into the country.

But the Catholic Church probably needs to re-look at some other areas. When a problem comes out in the country, a Catholic would be the last person to say something about it. This is one of the greatest weaknesses I find. When they should be screaming, "This is the teaching of the Church. This is what faith tells us."

Korby   They just don't speak out.

Woman   I have done a lot of campaigning about domestic violence for some years now. So I wrote to the Bishops' Conference . . .

Korby   Good.

Woman   . . . and asked them that I need a statement from you people to endorse what I'm doing. So they gave it. So I think they have changed their view toward divorce and cruelty in marriage. In terms of violence there could be a reason for the separation of the couple. Like you said, there are ways to go and directly ask for support. But, you know, I wish they could see it themselves.

Korby   Do it on their own initiative.

Woman   Yeah. Do it on their own initiative.

❖   ❖   ❖

Circumcision, Dowry, and the Ownership of Women

Circumcision and dowry are two ways in which many cultures perpetuate male ownership of women. Societies which practice female circumcision at the age of puberty mutilate the genitalia so that young females will neither enjoy nor desire sexual relations. In marriage, then, the woman will have no desire to seek a sexual relationship outside the marriage, but will be expected to submit to the husband's own desires. Dowry is another form of ownership. If the male pays dowry, he may assume that he owns the bride. If the bride's family pays dowry, the husband may continue to make financial demands or threaten the safety of his wife.

The Catholic Church maintains a distance from such arrangements, saying that they are cultural traditions over which it has no say. Yet in some cases, it is even customary for the Church to receive a percentage of dowry.

KENYA

Woman   We are looking especially at, uh, the purifying rituals. We feel that the women's natural processes are classified as impure. Why? It is God-given. God gives, you know, this gift of menstruation. Why is it impure?

Korby   Yeah, that's right.

Woman   And after giving birth you have to be purified. In order to receive sacraments or come back to church. And it's not only in the Church. But also in our traditions. When you come to puberty rites, the women again go through rituals, a special circumcision ritual. But for whose purpose?

Korby   Yeah.

Woman   I remember when I was growing up, when the girls are at the age of 13, 14, that's when they begin to realize that they are girls and they are women. There is a push in the village get them circumcised quickly. Why? To make sure there aren't those sexual urges. So they don't get pregnant before, you know, the marriage. And if a girl got pregnant before marriage it means her dowry will not be as much. So it was another economic kind of, uh, benefit, if she was a virgin.

And then [when she is married] she will never have a lover because she won't have the sexual urge, you know. And sometimes even the sexual act itself is very painful. And naturally they don't want it. It's just like an obligation they have to go through. So, like the man will know that she belongs to him, he can just go to her when he wants, and she can never go, and she can never even ask for sex. Because for a woman even to ask for sex, it is terrible, you know, traditionally.

Korby   Yeah.

Woman   And this is even being done today. You know, of course, there is this outcry when one girl dies because of the septic conditions that the girls are circumcised in, and then sometimes there is too much bleeding and they bleed to death. And certainly other kinds of complications may happen and the girls may die. And when they die, of course, it hits the news, and you see the men saying, "Oh, this is horrible." Even our president has condemned it. But actually, nobody has passed a law in this country to say that female circumcision is illegal. There is nothing like that. Why? Because it does not really affect men. And men are the ones who make the laws, you know?

Korby   If it's not a law that pertains to the men, they don't bother much about it.

Woman   No! And if a tradition, or a kind of a custom that is practiced, is good for the men, it will have to be protected, and they cry out, "It is our tradition." If a tradition is against the man, it will be abolished immediately. But if that tradition is against the woman, they say, "Oh, it's not good, yeah, yeah, but it is the tradition. It will die by itself.

KENYA

Woman   Men say a wife is property because, you know, after giving dowry, you belong, the woman belongs now to the man. They say it is only at "five" that a man is successful. And you know what that means?

Korby   Only at? . . .

Woman   Five.

Korby   Five?

Woman   Five. A man is successful when he has five things.

Korby   What are those five?

Woman   A girl, a doggie, a goat, a woman, a sheep.

Korby   Just put them right in with the animals.

Woman   But you know, Father, that is also in the Bible.

Korby   Sure it is! I was thinking that exactly. You know, it comes out in the commandments. Thou shalt not covet thy neighbor's wife, thou shalt not covet thy neighbor's goods.

NEW GUINEA

Korby   Is there a dowry system here?

Woman   It's a bride price. The man pays. And that's another big problem.

Korby   Then he probably figures she's . . .

Woman   And that's why some men beat their wives. Some say, "Well, we paid for them. They're our possession. We do what we like with them."

KENYA

Woman   The Church supports some of these things. They say, OK, we aren't going to marry you until you have gone through the traditional customs.

Korby   And what would be some of those traditional customs? What would they include?

Woman   One of them is to pay dowry. The husband has to pay a large sum of money or cattle or sheep and goats, whatever. From one ethnic community to another they have to pay. You know, in paying that property, the man then has this total kind of possession of the woman because he has paid. And therefore he becomes a kind of owner of the woman.

Korby   In a sense, he "bought" her.

Woman   Yeah. And actually some of them will say, "Who paid dowry for who in this house?" So the woman has to keep quiet and listen to the man whether he is right or he is wrong.

Korby	How is the amount of the dowry established?
Woman	OK, according to how educated the girl is. You know, for example, a girl who has gone up to the University level will cost much more than a girl who didn't have education. Traditionally, it was kind of a compliment. You know, they call it a covenant to make sure the wife will remain in the home and she will be protected. But today it has become a commercial thing. So they bargain, actually.

INDIA

Woman 1	A woman is forced to give money to a man at the time of marriage. We call it the dowry.
Korby	And that really comes from the family.
Woman 1	Yes. And that's one of the reasons why in India people don't want to have daughters. Because they say ultimately can we afford the dowry? That's one. The second thing is that the dowry business has become so bad that it now leads to a number of dowry deaths.
Korby	I've read about it in the States, yes.
Woman 1	That's right. The girl gets married, and the demands for more money don't stop with the marriage. They keep demanding more and more. And when the family cannot pay up, they would stage a "suicide," you know? And the commonest is fire. They just douse the woman with kerosene and set her on fire. And they say that it was a suicide. And nothing is said against it at all.

Woman 2   And the Church gets a certain percent.

Korby   Of the dowry?

Woman 1   I went to a particular area and I spoke to one of the priests regarding dowry, and he said, "Oh, this has been a tradition. It was started by the culture." And he asked me, "Who will come to me?" You know parents sometimes go to him and say, "Father, could you find a nice boy for my daughter?" And he said to me, "I don't get it [the percentage of dowry]. It goes for the upkeep of the Church.

    I said, "But Father, how can you take it? Because it means you are perpetuating dowry."

The Unapproachable Church

KENYA

Korby   There is a question I wanted to ask: If a woman has a marriage problem, why does the priest just tell her to go home and pray? Do you think that gives women the message that the priest is on the man's side?

Woman   No, I don't think that is the message. But I do think the message is that that's all you get from the Church. It's like what was said yesterday. I was very surprised yesterday when J said, "You can't talk to a sister about a lot of stuff." I mean, this is a Catholic woman saying that. I was really taken aback, you know? After that I reflected. I don't know if people know they can come to the Church as someone who is presently tired, someone who is presently angry, someone who is jealous. They feel they have to clean their act up, you know.

Korby   Yeah. Come to the church purified first.

Woman   Yeah. I was kind of startled.

Korby   I thought that the Church was supposed to be for sinners, for all sinners.

Woman   Yeah, but see I don't think we communicate that.

Local Priest   I was in Tanzania, and I was hearing confessions before Mass. I'm sitting under a tree, and a grandmother whom I know very well came up to me and tells me about how her grandchildren don't carry water for her, they don't bring her firewood. I'm listening to her, and I made an amazing mistake. I want to get that Mass started, you know, since it was getting late. So I said to her, "Do you have any sins?"

     She throws off her shawl — just a blanket — and shows me her breasts and says, "How can I sin? Look at me." I was stunned. I didn't know whether to laugh or to cry.

Korby   What did she mean by that?

Priest   Somehow we gave her the message that the only sin was impurity. You know? That was the sad part. And then she was insulted because she is an old lady, beyond that age. She was mad!

Korby   Is that right?

Priest   My intention was good. I took the wrong approach, of course. But the sad part was I think that's what she had heard all her life. We tend to emphasize certain things, perhaps, so sexuality would be to her the only sin. This was a real revelation to me about what an older Christian had picked up. So when I talked about sin, that is the connection she made, the only connection.

Education and Home-Life

The women explain that, traditionally, boys were educated before girls when money was tight. That is changing. Girls and women are becoming more educated, but they still face threatening situations at home and school. As important as education is in bringing about change, the root of change must begin in the home. Mothers must break the cycle of traditional roles and attitudes with their own children.

NEW GUINEA

Woman   We still have a long way to go, right from the primary school. If a couple has more than one child, and if they can't afford both, we know who goes to school. It's not the brightest of the two kids. It's the boy. And I can understand why they do that. Because in the village, in the land, it's the women who get married and go off to another clan. The boy stays on.

SOUTH AFRICA

Woman   With our kids, I think it is getting better. Sometimes with my own daughter, she blames me for not answering her father back.

Korby   Gradually getting better. Hmmm! Sure!

Woman "Why you not answer back?" (All laugh.) I was taught by my parents not to answer back.

Korby Sure.

Woman It is part of our culture.

Korby Where are your children picking up these ideas, to · go counter-culture?

[Several women speak at once]
At the university! I think education is . . .

Korby Aha! Again the education!

Woman Perhaps our children need apprenticeship. So I try not to discriminate between men's jobs and women's jobs. My son does the cleaning up of the house. Oh, sometimes he gripes about it.

Korby I used to gripe about it, too.

Woman So, I'm hoping that because this boy is doing the household chores, when he gets married, he will help his wife and children.

NEW GUINEA

Woman 1 When I first came to the country thirty-eight years ago, you had very few girls in school. And if they got beyond grade four, they were extraordinary. Because the people just didn't want the girls to go on. I mean they had, they had other things lined up for girls to do. It's not that they were against education or such. But by culture, the girls had other jobs to do that were more important. They didn't need education. And it's very difficult to break down that whole idea.

Nowadays, there are so many girls going through the schools and being highly educated, the men are feeling threatened. And that's adding to the aggressiveness.

Korby   And the increased wife-bashing, it seems.

Woman 1   Yes. Especially if the wife is an educated lady.

Korby   Uh huh.

Woman 1   When our committee came over in the 60s, we were asked to come and help, um, educate the girls. Especially the girls. Because culturally the priests weren't even supposed to be talking to them.

Korby   Jeepers.

Woman 1   You could talk to them on the road or something. But they couldn't go to their homes, and sit down with them, and so on.

And even today, a lot of women don't want to go to the university, the teachers' training college, because of the morals there. You know, the men force their way into the rooms at night. Anyway, they're really frightened to go. You have to be a really strong woman in order to be able to fight things off.

Korby   One woman mentioned that what we need to do to get to the root of the difficulty as soon as possible is to have the mothers in the homes, when they are raising their children, not pass on the traditional kind of training which puts the boys up here and the girls here. You know? Because the mothers are very, very influential in indicating, "No, boys don't do that. And girls don't do this."

Woman 1   Yeah. Well, I think it's got to come over a period of generations, you know.

Korby   In a certain sense, I guess, would it be true that it's almost going to be necessary for the women in the village to try to get the girls to see that when they marry, they sort of break the tradition of training the boys to be dominant and the girls to be submissive?

Woman 2   Yes, that's one thing. They always learn to the boy, "You can do this. You can beat your sister up and your sister won't beat you back." It's the mother who's letting this happen. She must say right from the start, "No, I will not let my daughter be pushed down."

Korby   What is it that priests in the Church can do to make it better? Do you have any ideas?

Woman 2   Yes. I think in homilies they should stress more on the wife and the family. Tell the women more that she has to start right in her family to educate her children.

Korby   And that way they could get the ideas across to the women who can't read and who haven't gone to school. They will hear it.

Woman 2   That's right, yes.

Korby   And they will come to know about it. But it has to be said again and again and again, huh?

KENYA

Woman 1   In the African culture, the boys are brought up to
            have that attitude. So the mothers kind of help the
            boys have that attitude.

Woman 2   And to change that, then it has to start with the par-
            ents. If, like right now I know that we are equal, that
            we can also make a decision, then I bring up my
            daughter with that knowledge. Then my daughter
            will grow up knowing that she has a right, that she
            can also be heard. But if my husband and I only lis-
            ten to my son, then there is a difference. My daugh-
            ter will grow up thinking that it is only what the boy
            says that should be done.

Woman 1   It's interesting the way the Church will step in, too,
            and say, well, that's African tradition, and if that's
            the culture and that's the place of men and that's the
            place of women in the society, we can't touch that.
            But the Church doesn't look at bigamy in the same
            way. And that's also a tradition. So it's that kind of
            convenient ambivalence that you see so many times.

UGANDA

Korby   Where did you get your ideas that it ought to be dif-
            ferent?

Woman   At school! Because now even in school we talk about
            these things.

Korby   Uh-huh!

Woman   And again, I think our participating in different ac-
            tivities has brought us into discussion with other
            women in different places, from different traditions,
            where we discuss these issues. You are definitely in-

fluenced by the various changes that have taken place at different times in different places. Education was something that was traditionally denied us until recent years.

PHILIPPINES

Woman   You see, there is a difference of bringing a hope to marriage. In the past, we look to our husbands to make the decisions, and then he consults us. But you see, with the Western type of education we are having, especially with the younger generation, women are asking for equality. When I got married thirty-four years ago, women were supposed to be submissive. With the current education that we have — my husband was educated in college, I was also educated in college — when it comes to decision-making in the home we discuss it, so there is equality in our house. Whatever decision we make, it will be a decision between us.

NEW GUINEA

Korby   Is most of the female population literate, or illiterate?

Woman   Illiterate.

Korby   In your own particular case, how was it that you were able to get your education, and to get to the point to recognize it, to be aware, and so on?

Woman   I am thankful that my family is very understanding. My parents and everybody supported me, not caring if I was a woman or a man. They said, "She's got the brains, she goes. We pay."

Korby   Good.

Woman   Sometimes along the way I thought I wasn't good enough. I said, "I'm coming home." My uncle said, "You stupid girl, stay there and go to school."

Korby   That's great. You were kind of down in the dumps at the time, huh?

Woman   Yes.

Korby   I imagine you ran into a lot of obstacles and road-blocks at the time?

Woman   Yes. The whole village that I come from, they were saying to my mother, "What are you doing sending this girl to school? She is going to come back pregnant, come back with. . . . "I mean, it's just the way people are thinking. They are just afraid of this. Socially or traditionally, people have never sent their daughter this far.

Korby   So I'm just wondering, has it been your experience that priests and sisters have, uh, in general helped to overcome the inequalities that are in society? Or have they perpetuated the inequality? What was your experience? Did they help you to develop, you know, as you would like to?

Woman   Yes, they . . . generally speaking, yes they have. I've been through mission schools all my life, so I can't really say anything about the other side, but they have really helped me come this far.

❖   ❖   ❖

The Politics of Fear

KENYA

Woman 1   Professor X, the environmentalist, is a Catholic sister. But, OK, whatever she is crusading for is, I
mean, she does it on her own. Really, she's worked
very hard. When she was attacked, nobody from the
Church said anything. These controversial people,
we don't know them. And I think that is wrong.
They should find identity also in the Church.

Korby   In other words they need support groups.

Woman 1   She was told publicly, from the highest voice in this
country, that women have no right to speak in this
area. Now the Church could have picked up on that.
It would have been an opportunity, I would say, for
the Church to be supportive and say that the Church
would have a view on the rights of women, and we
would object to the statement that on questions of
environment and the quality of life, that women
have no voice.

Korby   There were no reporters that picked up on that?

Woman 1   Mercifully, they didn't crucify the Church. She stuck
out her neck and she fought that battle and she won,
eventually. And the people who came to her support
were the international community. Now it's a shame,
here we are, we are Kenyans and then we throw our
own person out in the cold.

Korby   How in the world can we change that?

Woman 1   We can first of all clean up our own act as members of the Church. Because even within our own Church I think we are fighting for power. People would like to be bishops, so priests will not want to talk because in case, you know, they are to become the next bishop, because we have still expatriated bishops, eh?

Woman 2   Part of the problem is that many of the bishops can discipline very quickly, especially in Kenya. They call in the Mother Superior and he tells the Mother Superior to discipline her sister. And they do.

Woman 3   He told the woman to discipline her.

Woman 1   And they did. They said it and, well, she was called very many names. But she stuck her neck out and she stood her ground.

Korby   Yeah. There is definitely a need to be careful here, because if you are here for a while the security is just unbelievable. Oh, unbelievable. You must be very careful. We can talk here, but when you are talking like this in a restaurant, you know, about the government or anything, you don't know who is security. You can get picked up or thrown out of the country right away. Now *we* will just get thrown out of the country. The local people are the ones who can just disappear.

Woman 1   Killed.

Woman 2   So people are justifiably afraid, because if the foreign minister of the country can just be brutally killed — the second or third most powerful person in the country — how about the ordinary little person like us? So people are aware of that.

Korby	So the bishops are somewhat conscious, rightfully so, but they are overly conscious, I think, you know? And they are afraid. They don't know what their role is, really. A little example of that. I tried to get a meeting with the cardinal just to explain to him the little meetings we had for the first time of a small Christian justice and peace group. I was with two lay people who were part of the group, and he said, "Well, this isn't supposed to be about politics." Right away: poor, politics — danger.
Woman 2	See, that's the fear. If you are not under the Church umbrella you can't say anything. So that's why the Church here has to encourage and protect these forums at this time.

Religion: The Realm of Women

KENYA

Woman	I have always wondered what the women can really do in the Church. And to stop feeling inferior in the society. Yet, when I tell my husband, "Let's go to the church," he tells me sometimes, "That is only for women and children."
Korby	Do you think that homilies on this subject of treating people with equal dignity, equal respect, and giving everybody the opportunity to bring out, to develop the potential of the gifts they have, would that help? Would men listen to the homilies that are given that way? Or would they quit going to Church?!
Woman	They do not go to Church.

SOUTH AFRICA

Woman 1   You must educate the men as well. "Look guys, this is how it is!" This is the thing! And it seems to me, in this area alone, who is coming to Mass? The women! Where are the men? I mean, why aren't they hearing the message?

Korby   Do the fathers in the parish do anything to get the men to come? Write a letter to the men and invite them to come, or something like that?

Woman 1   Sometimes the priest feels reluctant to invite them.

Korby   That's right. Many men, it seems, think that religion and going to church — that's a woman's job. At Mass this morning, Fr. Dave and I concelebrated. It was the end of the term, and the students were to be there. I think there were about four times as many girls as boys! And actually in the school it was about equal. So I'm wondering what happened. Why would the girls have come as they did, and they were the ones who had to stay and help clean the place! The boys didn't have that job.

Woman 2   That's interesting. Because we have a prayer meeting on the seventh of the month. And the kids who come to our prayer meeting are thirty girls and one boy. And yet the kids who come from the villages to the [night-time] prayer meeting are mostly boys.

Korby   Is that right? Do you have any idea what accounts for that?

Woman 2   Parents won't let their girls run out in the night somewhere, where they don't know where they are going. They try to keep control of that. But the boys are brave enough to go out.

Korby   So if there were the same freedom for both, the girls would be there?

Woman 1   Yes.

Korby   If there weren't the dangers for the girls.

Woman 1   If it was during the day, the girls would come.

Woman 2   The people of the villages are deeply religious here. I am an English teacher, and the feedback I get from the girls is "The best day of my entire life was the day of my First Communion. That was the most wonderful day of my life. And I would be very happy on Christmas because it is Jesus' birthday. So we hear religion from the girls, but we don't hear it from the boys. We hear a little bit, but not quite as much. But boys are interested in other things, you know? "I really want a car," that sort of stuff.

NEW GUINEA

Woman 1   Your question here, to do with women, how we can contribute towards the Church. I would say that the women have much more to contribute to the Church than maybe anybody else. It is us women that keep holding up the faith in our own families.

Korby   Really.

Woman 1   You see, the husbands will drive their wives and kids to church. And they go back and sit outside and wait.

Woman 2   Our men folk really need a lot of . . .

Woman 1   A lot of help.

Woman 2   Spiritual help. And yet the men, men is running the show. The men is deciding. I mean the men is running the show within the Church and the government both.

Woman 1   But we don't, we aren't worried about who is running it. I am not going to church because a priest, this priest is saying the Mass. I'm going there because Jesus is there.

Building Self-Confidence

SOUTH AFRICA

Korby   You mentioned having seminars.

Woman   You know, I think us women need to get our self-confidence. Right now we are not confident, because we are always leaning behind the men. So most of the time if we are at a meeting or what, we are sometimes afraid to voice our views, because always, the man has to say everything and the woman has just to keep quiet.

Korby   And probably there are so many men and you are just a few in those meetings. And after a while you hear people talking, that gets you all the time, and you say, "Well, I wonder if I *am* right." To help build that self-confidence, yes.

Woman   Yes.

Korby   I was talking with the women yesterday evening right after we got here. I was so tired that I could hardly see straight, but they had been waiting since 5 o'clock. Those women seemed to be really hungry for some kind of workshops and seminars to be able to learn how to be leaders in society. They said, "We don't have any education. We don't know how." Are there some people who would be able to teach them how to be leaders in a group, something of that nature? Maybe there should be something like that for women?

Woman   That's true, because some of the African parents never went to school, but some are educated. Some can come in and hold a workshop and make people aware. And sometimes we don't use our gifts because we are women. "I cannot do this. I am keeping my gifts back, because I am a woman.

Korby   That's probably another thing. This whole thing of having been *put down* for so long, that women often will not feel really . . . well, not have a good sense of self-identity, self-confidence.

NEW GUINEA

Woman   Women don't have the freedom to speak out what they feel. Sometimes they are scared. Even when they see that their husband has done something wrong, they don't really tell their husbands, "What you have done is wrong" because they are scared their husband will beat them.

Korby   Sure. And as a result they don't feel good about themselves. And they're very quiet and so forth. I've noticed that with some of the women in Africa. I think it comes from acting so timid. So timid that when I'd ask them what their name is, I'd have to get right up, right next to their lips to find out what their name was. You know? Because they'd talk so quiet. They didn't have any self-confidence because of the fact that they keep getting beat down all the time.

SRI LANKA

Woman   A number of priests called on me to do some talks on prayer, and then one of them called me to do a retreat instead of a priest. I was really reluctant. I have worked with small groups, never big. I know the minds of men. Many would not accept it. I had no courage. It is unfortunate that we still have this attitude in the Church.

Korby   You experienced it within yourself?

Woman   That's right. I have now four years of theology, and I was studying more, and with all these experiences I had to be under many men. You understand? Because they are men.

Korby   On the one hand you had to be under them, and yet on the other hand when somebody asked you to do something you were reluctant.

PHILIPPINES

Woman	The women have to learn to be more aggressive. I think, perhaps, if you want to get on top of any high rank you do have to be aggressive.
Korby	Yeah. That's the unfortunate thing. You kind of have to pick up the bad things that the men have in order to get on with it.
Woman	You can't cry, and you can't do this. You can't show where being female comes in.

Narrative Two
Woman at Seminary

(A woman in Kenya depicts an experience in an American seminary course, and an experience in her native Kenya.)

Woman   I remember this particular teacher came into the class and he looked around. I happened to be the only woman in the class, and the only African, the only black. So he said, "Sister, are you sure you are in the right class?"

I said, "I think I am." I was supposed to be in this course.

And then he said, "This is a very difficult course. I don't know whether you will be able, you know, whether you have that systematic mind to handle it."

My first reaction was, oh, maybe he looked at my previous performance and he was not impressed. But actually my previous performance had all been so good. There was no question about my performance.

So I was talking to some of the women and they said, "That's what we are talking about. You should learn. They don't think women can think. They don't think women have got a systematic mind. And there, you know, you have to fight. It is like you have to prove that you are able to do this all the time."

That was like the awakening. The moment of realization, oh-ho! Actually, I had to work so hard for that particular course to make sure I didn't, you know, do badly. I did well, actually. So thank God for that. But I had to work extra hard for that purpose.

So that's how my own personal awareness was awakened. And I began to get involved in the women's groups and learn more about what was going on, you know, in the American scene. And then I would read, you know, the African material.

So when I came back to Africa, of course I was very sensitive to issues. And when I went to school here there were just two other women. I wrote a paper on the images of women in African traditional religion. I just wanted to expose the whole reality of abuse in the name of tradition.

I am telling you the men got so mad. They said, "How did you do this? Are you sure that this is correct?"

Everything was documented. So I said, "You can prove me wrong, but it is here, documented. I have done research, and this is what I have heard. This is an academic paper, and I am ready to be quoted without being afraid because it is what it is."

Chapter Three

The Ministry of Women

Exclusion and Ministry

To suggest that women be allowed to "do more" is itself an insult, suggests one woman. Women have given and given and given. The question is, What kinds of ministry will be open to women? Although the women interviewed feel the sting of exclusion, many sense that change is occurring. Sometimes change is painfully slow, or inconsistent.

WEST SENECA, NEW YORK

Woman 1   I know you don't mean it this way, because I have worked with you for a long time. But even to say, "let women do more" is a knife to my heart. Honest to goodness. And I know you don't mean it. But I know I can say it in front of you.

Korby   Sure you can!

Woman 1   But that's the attitude you get. I'm being . . . it almost brings me to tears, that's how strong it is in me. But there is a lot of attitude that comes across that says, "I'll let you do this."

Woman 2   But that isn't ministry. Ministry should be gospel response. It should be response to Christ. That's what we are supposed to be about. And if the attitude is "I'm doing Father favors" or "I'm helping him do his work," that isn't ministry.

Korby   That was the kind of thing I picked up from Ladora when we were working together, you know. She really got hurting a lot of times from the way she would get put down, especially by some of the European priests.

UGANDA

Woman   Christianity treated women in the same manner as the culture. The woman was supposed to be behind the curtains or supposed to sit on that side of the pew, and the women were not even allowed near the sanctuary because she was not holy, I suppose. I don't know. But when it came to cleaning the church, the women had to appear and do it.

KENYA

Woman   Every time I have to fight them. Especially language. I'm so much sensitive especially of the sexist language. And every time, I don't spare anybody. Anybody who breaks, who uses that language and talks about the salvation of all men. And I say, "Please, why do you want to alienate me from this discussion? I am part of this discussion. So please would you use an inclusive language so that I am a part of it?" So of course they want to kind of trivialize it. But it has sometimes been very painful.

SRI LANKA

Woman   There are some people whom we have educated. Recently I sent a paper to Father, I wrote "his." But I saw him putting a stroke and writing "her." Now that shows he is thinking. So like that there are people who have taken up our cause.

NEW GUINEA

Woman   The language in the offices and sermons and that. They think it's such a little thing, "Why worry when they say, 'God came to save all men.'?" They say it doesn't matter. It does matter! I say, "You are saying it does not matter what I feel. And I feel excluded!"

SRI LANKA

Korby   Do the clergy in general help to develop situations in which women become more aware of their God-given right to be able to develop their potential more?

Woman   They are doing. The young priests, they are doing.

Korby   Yeah, right. Father . . . I imagine, for instance, is pretty open to the . . .

Woman   Very open. Very open. But he is also prudent.

Korby   Yeah. And he ought to be prudent. You have to be, have to keep moving, but not to stir up the higher-ups too much.

Woman   And you must know where to draw the line.

Korby   Right. To say we can't push any further now.

UGANDA

Woman   When you greet a man you must kneel down. The man doesn't kneel for the woman.

Korby   When it gets to the point where they both kneel to each other, then we'll have some equality.

Woman   The woman now must always kneel.

Korby   I noticed one thing that could be changed. I noticed a couple of the sisters came in to talk to the archbishop while we were in there, and they came in and knelt down and bowed and they were on their knees all the while they were talking to him.

Woman   Yes.

Korby   Now, I would think that would be a case where he would say, "Sister, that's fine. Stand up and let's talk."

Woman   Yes, OK. That takes a bit of time. Besides, the religious are told they must be humble. That has been their upbringing. Now, the bishop, much as he may want. . . .

Korby   Might not be able to change it?

Woman   Might not be able to change it so fast. Our archbishop here is a man that I know, we grew up in the same area. He is very simple and definitely doesn't call for that.

Korby   Yes, I didn't think that he did. It was not that he called for it. They just did it.

Woman   But many of our leaders, they are coming to realize that they've got to also participate in the process of bringing about change.

PHILIPPINES

Korby   Have you experienced that kind of, oh, an attitude of being looked down upon in the Church?

Woman   No. Because here in the Philippines, I think maybe the women are very much involved in the Church activities and the spiritual activities. And the priests and the hierarchy know that. It's the women who make these things move. So it's not the men, because the men are too busy with making money, you know, other things. Ordinarily, the men in the family just leave it all to the women when it comes to morality, discipline, and religious life. Of course, there are exceptions, husbands who belong to some religious organizations who take the lead in, you know, jumping in and addressing their spiritual side.

Fr. Dave   What do you think has influenced the men in those cases to take the initiative, to be more involved?

Woman   I think it's because of the women. The women, the wives. They see an enormous change in the wives. So somehow, because of this change in the women, some men are enlightened. And their eyes are opened. There must be something good that this wife of mine is doing.

NEW GUINEA

Woman In the 1960s, when our sisters first went to a very remote areas in Seven Highlands, at Mass on Sunday the men would be sitting down cross-legged in Church. And the women would have to crawl in order to keep their heads lower than the men's. So it's come a long way. Now you have women catechists in that area.

SOUTH AFRICA (HIGH SCHOOL)

Young I think the Church can really help if Apartheid can
Woman 1 be abolished in *it* first. One year they were having a big feast here. When it was time to eat, they separated the blacks and the colored. They called them to eat separate. They were all everywhere, and one person said to a black, "Don't touch me!"

Korby So those are situations where the Church could lead as an example. I noticed in church, too, the boys are on one side and the girls on the other. Is that discrimination? Does that help or does it hinder?

Young It's for singing.
Woman 2

Korby Why can't you sit together?

Young For singing.
Woman 2

Korby   For singing, well, yes. But that's not the way it started.

Fr. Dave   Also, what about on Sunday Masses? On Sunday you see the men sitting on the left and the women sitting on the right. Why don't the husbands sit with the wives?

Young   They are shy?
Woman 2

ENGLAND

Woman   Shall I say I think that when we talk about women priests we are up against a major obstacle there. It's just a dead end. But let's then have another look at what women really do, what the Church would do without them, really.

Korby   Yeah. Have things gotten better from your point of view since Vatican II? And if so, in what way? Has it gotten worse, in what ways?

Woman 1   I think that we, ourselves, haven't been assertive enough about our role in the Church. And while there are priests in parishes who, you know, have a very hard-line approach to the role of women in the Church, there are a lot of priests who, like yourself, acknowledge that we have a contribution to make. I have encouraged women altar servers, girl altar servers. And I found that it came to a very serious end in the parish I worked in.

Korby   End in what respect? You were stopped?

Woman 1   Some parishioners led a protest and said that all the altar servers would resign if the practice didn't stop.

And there is the Cardinal with his four bishops, and thousands of priests and thousands of altar servers, as many girls as boys, which acknowledges their role in the church. But it just came to a dead end like that (in our parish). I thought, what is the point of pursuing it, you know? You have to live in a parish. Sometimes we have to compromise.

Woman 2   Father, I think that women, dedicated women with a love of service, I think that the Church treats them coldly at times, doesn't it? Sometimes where there is a woman there is life.

Korby   I noticed that myself working with Ladora. Because my outlook is sometimes, "Well, we've got to get this done, let's do it," and so forth. And some people are maybe going to get their nose rubbed in the mud a bit. But she would always come up with that feeling for the individual person, you know, the nurturer of life more than I. I said, hey, we've got to have more of that in the Church itself.

Woman 1   Can I ask one thing? In your travels around, are there some countries that strike you as having made more progress than others in this field? Obviously America has.

Korby   Some parts of America. And in general, I suppose, so have you (in England).

Woman 1   I don't think as much as you.

Korby   No. But it varies so much from diocese to diocese and from parish to parish. And yes, it depends an awful lot on the bishop. You have some bishops who operate under the principle of "don't ask me any questions because if you ask me I will have to say no." And so people begin to catch on and they just go ahead. That can create problems when another bishop comes in and says, "Golly, no!" The places that I have noticed in the United States are mostly within Wisconsin, Minnesota, up in that north central area where there are sisters who handle the whole parish except the sacramental aspects. But my question is, how much of this is coming because of the fact that there aren't males to do the work? It's a matter of necessity rather than principle.

Woman   We've got it sort of fixed in our minds that the Church is run by priests. The priests are provided with civil service, and whatever you want to know, you go get it from the priest. You might have the parish council which advises the priest, but he's got the checkbook. The position of the laity in the parish sometimes is sort of pushed to one side. "You are not very welcome in this, except we want you to work in the schools, of course, because we couldn't do that."

SOUTH AFRICA (HIGH SCHOOL)

Korby   What are the things that you would like to be able to do in the Church? Well, you said be ordained. That will come, I think, sooner or later, probably later. But what are other things that you as a woman would like to do right now in the Church, that you can not do? Now they let you scrub the floor, wash the windows and fix the flowers. What do you think you should be able to do?

           (Silence.)

Korby   Anybody got any ideas?

*Young
Woman*   I think there is discrimination because boys are the
           ones who serve Mass and we can't.

NEW GUINEA

Woman   Some men, I think, find it easier to approach a
           woman if they want to go to confession. We used to
           go out to the villages sometimes. And often people
           came and said, "Sister, why don't you hear confes-
           sion?"

Korby   Yeah. I know one country where there is just kind of
           an informal understanding where the sisters are
           really handling parishes, period. In doing counsel-
           ing, there are a lot of people who just, in effect what
           they are doing is going to confession to the sisters.
           But they don't want to repeat it to a priest because
           they don't really know them that well. So what the
           sister will do is contact the priest and say this person
           wants to go to confession. It's OK, I know everything
           that's in it. It's OK, just give her absolution. Or just
           give him absolution. That's what they do.

ENGLAND

Woman 1   There are a lot of women who wouldn't want to go
           to a woman for confession. They would much rather
           go to a priest. Well, they put themselves down
           sometimes.

Korby   OK.

Woman 2   It's because of the culture.

Woman 1   Well, women are too perceptive. We want to see a man, he doesn't understand half of it!

Korby   Then they can get away with it, huh?! That is why some of us in the seminary chose a deaf priest! He won't know what is going on in the least.

SRI LANKA

Woman   The present Sri Lanka Church wants to experiment with certain parishes given over totally to female pastorship of Sisters to see how they manage. Except for the absolute need, like for Mass. For that, if there is to be a Eucharistic celebration, we can get a priest from somewhere. People suffer a lot because when a priest shuttles between one Mass and another, sometimes people in the fold lose devotion.

Korby   Yeah.

Woman   Many non-Catholic Christian groups recognize and give a place to the females. In the Roman Catholic Church it has to come up in a big way still. But the Church is beginning to recognize. That, I think, was spelled out to me just last week when we were try-ing to open a new parish. The idea was thrown, "What do you think, Sister, if we try to give an entire parish to be totally run by Sisters? I think we should experiment with it."

Korby   Terrific! And then the Sisters will probably be able to help to develop a lay leadership in the parish.

Woman   Yeah. Because I think we have not been able to ana-lyze and show the people that where evangelization is concerned, the laity takes first place, religious second, and the priest third.

Korby   So right now it's reversed from what it really should be.

❖   ❖   ❖

NEW GUINEA

Korby   What are your ideas about, you know, the status of women in the Church?

Woman   You know, it has improved a lot. I mean, before it was absolutely nothing. There's an example in our diocese. A woman with a family of six children has been the diocesan education secretary, running the diocesan education office for about ten years. Now, she's had bishops who have had a lot of trust in her. So she can go ahead and do things. I think the element of trust has to be developed a lot more toward women. In what I am doing now, I really feel the bishop is trusting me.

Korby   Trust. Have confidence put in them.

Woman   But I worry about what ideas are passed on to priests in the seminary.

❖   ❖   ❖

ENGLAND

Woman 1   As I was saying to these fellows tonight, if you were to look at the head office in Rome, the section concerned with religious, you won't find a single woman in the head office in charge of all women religious. Maybe there are some there. It is possible that it has changed a little bit. But mostly they are all monsignors of this sort or the other. And that makes me nervous, you know?

Woman 2   When there is change, a lot of times it happens because they haven't got the priests available. It's a stop-gap thing rather than an ideal. So they put women in positions as a last resort.

Woman 1   It is very difficult in the family when the boy can be an altar server and the girl can't. How can you explain that to the girls? There is no rationale. We just ask them to accept something you can't really justify.

Woman 2   Years ago the girls used to have to wear something on their heads. Remember when the woman went into church she always had her head covered, and the boys didn't?

Local Priest   Do you think the change is at hand? The fact that there is more women's involvement, is it coming out of the fact that the priests are in a stop-gap situation, or is it really a recognition of women as persons with rights and gifts and talents that have not been recognized? Why is it happening now? I just think of myself in terms of the breviary. You know, I get furious sometimes with the men, and you know, twenty years ago that wouldn't have bothered me. Why is it bothering me now? Is it just because of the movement, and what has happened to bring this movement about?

INDIA

Korby   What is it that you can do in the Church? Can you distribute communion now?

Woman   Communion we don't, Father.

Korby   Uh huh, Father will do that. OK, can the women be on committees in the Church? Do they lead Bible study groups and things like that?

Woman   Yeah. We lead the Gospel and explain it. And give guidance to the people, and when they want to receive First Holy Communion, we give them guidance. We say about Jesus, how to receive him. Help them go for Act of Contrition, and when they go to confession, how to confess all your sins. Many of them, old patients, they are about to die, you know. Me, I will help them to have a good death.

INDIA

Korby   It's, uh, all I can say is it's very interesting. I guess the Holy Spirit knows what he is doing.

Woman   What she is doing!

Korby   What she is doing, yes! Right! Very good! The Catholic Church goes on because of the Spirit. Because of the Holy Spirit in the people.

Ordination

Women speak with many different voices on the subject of ordination. Some do not equate equality of ministry with sameness of ministry, and therefore do not seek ordination; there are other kinds of ministry, and these should be afforded the same kind of respect as the priesthood. Others view ordination as an imperative, a calling extended to many women by God, to which access has been denied by men. A third perspective comes from those who do not seek ordination for women precisely because they believe the priesthood is part of a hierarchical structure which they see as the root of exclusion in the first place.

WEST SENECA, NEW YORK

Woman 1   I don't think everyone who's a sister, who belongs to a religious community, has aspirations, or even needs and wants to be a priest. Do you think I am right in believing that?

Korby   Definitely.

Woman 1   I am disturbed about the strident women who are waving the old flag for ordination, and I'm thinking, are they going to be kind, generous, gentle people?

Korby   Well, those particular individuals would be screened out in a situation of that type, just as. . . .

Woman 2   Forgive me, Father Korby, do you suppose, on the other side of the fence, we have screened out all of the men who are not kind and gentle?

Korby   No, I don't suppose so.

Woman 2   I think that the ministry of priesthood needs to be redefined.

Korby   What is a priest? What is a priest thought of in the Church, or what was Christ's idea of a priest?

Woman 2   I think that we have held on to too many of the me-
dieval notions of priests being, um, being an ele-
vated superior being.

Korby   Uh-huh.

Woman 2   I think a valid question to ask as you travel, too, is
"What do you think that the feminine experience
would bring to the priesthood?" Because I think that
as it is now, you eliminate half of the human experience from the priesthood by not having women as a
part of it.

INDIA

Korby   So what can we do to try to bring about some greater
equality faster than it is? Change is slowly coming
because more women are getting an education. But
is there anything that you can see that would help
make the process faster? Are there any suggestions
that you would have for priests and bishops?

Woman   Yeah. There is now a shortage of priests, and there
are many places without priests where sisters and
other lay people are doing much of the work. But
why can't they allow sisters to be ordained?

Korby   Yeah, I wish I knew. That's one of the things that
Father Dave and I were wondering about. Just how
many women really are thinking about that and
wanting to work toward being ordained? Because
there are people in the Church who are saying that
it's only women in the United States and Canada
and a couple of places in Europe who are expressing
the desire to have a Church where women would be
ordained. But what we are finding is that there are

women in all the countries that we have been in who expressed that same idea.

So maybe that's one thing that can be done is if the women around the world keep asking the question, "Why can't we be ordained?" And still keep asking, asking, asking, asking, and praying. You know? Yeah, just like it says in the Gospel, somebody comes to the door and the guy's in bed and, uh, he knocks at the door and he doesn't answer. Finally he answers because he is just getting tired of being pestered. So maybe that's one thing that we have to do. Just sort of a ground swell of asking why, why, why.

❖ ❖ ❖

SRI LANKA

Korby   Are there sisters who believe that Christ intended that eventually women should be ordained, too?

Woman 1   No, no. Not so important.

Korby   There are other things which are more basic that need to be taken care of first?

Woman 2   The bishops say that women's ordination would kill ordination. I said, "I won't be a priest, but I am ready to fight for the cause."

Korby   Uh-huh. Are there other women religious who have the same belief?

Woman 2   There are some of us who are of this opinion, but we are only a small minority that can be counted on your fingers.

❖ ❖ ❖

SOUTH AFRICA (HIGH SCHOOL)

Young Woman 1	I see that only the men are priests. They are the only ones who work at church. I don't see any women doing it.
Korby	So you think that women should be ordained priests?
Young Woman 1	Yes. Given a chance to choose the will of God.
Korby	So you think that some young women are being called by God to be priests, but that can't be because of the rules of the Church? Is that it?
Young Woman 1	Yes, yes.
Korby	OK. Are there some of you disagree with — and some who agree with her, or some who say, "Mm, I never thought about that"?
Young Woman 2	I never thought about that.

KENYA

Korby	You shook your head before when I asked about ordination.
Woman 1	I did, but see what I was saying before about structures? When you say, what would equality mean, like what positions? So many women that I know aren't interested in the positions. It's an unequal structure to start with.

Korby   Yes, that's right.

Woman 1   So to buy into that and just say, I mean, that any position is open, no, that doesn't make any basic change for human liberation, human equality. So to be ordained into that kind of structure, what, where would that lead?

Korby   Would there be, among the Kenyan sisters, some who think that the equality which we're talking about would include ordination and positions of the clergy in the Church?

Woman 2   There are few. But in Kenya, we don't have highly educated sisters.

Korby   Yeah, they just don't think of it.

Woman 2   When you begin talking about these things, they don't understand what you are talking about, and therefore you end up totally parallel, and you are called names like "radical, she wants to do crazy things."

Korby   A radical feminist. May I ask, what do you think? Do you think it should be that women are ordained?

Woman 2   Yes, that is good. That is good, yes.

Korby   You are a sister here?

Woman 2   Yes. Traditionally, in African culture women were priests. If you go with our traditions, that is one area where there was no discrimination, in religious leadership. Because they saw religious leadership as inspired by God. And individuals, like, if they felt they were being called in a dream, in a vision, you know. And if a young girl felt that God was calling her in a vision to be a priest, she became a priest because the people respected that.

SOUTH AFRICA

Korby   Sometimes I have heard a priest say, "We can't have the girls serving Mass because then they will be wanting to be ordained." So I just say to them, "Well, what's wrong with that?" But I'm just wondering, what do you ladies think about that? Do you think that women ought to be ordained?

Woman   That is a difficult question. Yes, but I don't know if they will make it. You know, Jesus was a man. He dies on the cross with his life. The priest raises his hands in a particular fashion during the consecration, and a woman can't do that? If she could only rise with Christ on the cross. . . .

Korby   Wow! Just a little bit of homemade scripture, homemade theology!

KENYA

Woman   All over the world, the people you have met. How do they feel about women priests?

Korby   It depends upon what country you are in as to how many do and how many don't. There again it is a cultural kind of thing. I would say in the United States — I am trying to give an estimate — lay people, it would be about 50% would think that equality should include ordination. With the priests, I honestly can't tell you. I really don't know. There are, I would say, maybe 25-30% of the priests.

Woman   From my past experience, all nuns, the majority I've met in different places talk often of women always supposed to be submissive.

Korby   Not the nuns in the United States.

Woman   You see, we are putting our case to the priests and hoping for the nuns to come and assist us. But if they are not there, then we may not reach our target. Then we are likely to go whoosh!

NEW GUINEA

Korby   Over in the United States, there are different groups who are all pushing for ordination.

Woman   Yeah. Personally, I am not at all interested in women's ordination. I do not want to be another club member in the system that promotes oppression. I am looking for equal participation. Equality of ministry. I do not what to wear a dog collar. But I do want to see that as a person called by Christ, I have the right and I have the call to minister to others as a full woman. And I don't have to apologize that I am a woman. And I don't have to aim to be a man in a man's society. People who get all keyed up about ordination are not really looking at what women are saying, what women are feeling, how women are being treated.

Exodus

The women tell Fr. Korby that young women are leaving the Catholic Church because they do not find a role for themselves within, and find that the church does not minister to their needs.

KENYA

Woman 1   I have a suspicion that women are caught somewhere in the middle. The Church wants you to remain . . .

Woman 2   . . . removed.

Woman 1   Yes, they want you to remain as a prayer group, with, you know, the right songs on a big occasion, or wearing nice flowing robes. There. That's it.

Woman 2   I don't think even our bishops know what women are thinking.

Woman 1   They can't.

Korby   Do they want to know?

Woman 1   I don't think they want to know.

Korby   What percentage of Catholic women, would you say, would have the same general feelings and ideas that you are expressing here?

Woman 1   I think it must be a big group. I'm talking about the experience of my generation.

Korby   Sure, yeah.

Woman 1   I mean, I know people who laugh and say, ah, there is nothing, really, in the Church for people like us. Say, ah, maybe we are too young, or they say it doesn't make sense anyway. So they are dropping out, and I know we are having an exodus of young people from the Church. They are moving on to these charismatic groups where they can shout and sing, and they can speak and they are heard. To be young and to be a Catholic, it is very difficult.

Korby   Because they don't see much in the way of a future. For their ideas, and, uh, for a greater human rights and equality, and being listened to, and all that.

Woman 2   I wanted to say that there are women who could say something, but the problem is they just become reluctant.

Korby   Yes. Why waste my time?

Woman 2   I know they are there. Even if you talk and are not harmed, you feel that it . . . it is useless. It is better I keep quiet.

Korby   You just feel rejected.

Woman 3   I had an opportunity to meet a professional woman, a doctor, who caused quite an uproar among the priests. She was trying to explain to a certain priest that nobody in the Church wants to talk about single parents and their children. Single mothers. They are there. I know a support group at, um, Saint Paul Chapel. I don't think anybody else is doing that. Some priests are very heavy-hearted. There is no open policy for these people. They are trying to push the problem under the rug. It is ready to explode.

Korby   Yes, I know for many priests the matter of single
            mothers is a big problem. I have heard it said by
            priests that if we encourage them and have support
            groups, we are encouraging prostitution. And, uh,
            maybe even some of your married men and women
            will say that.

            I think that the point there is that the Church
            doen't even want to face some of the basic problems
            of women. They don't know how to face them. They
            are afraid of them.

KENYA

Woman   There are many of us who might have developed
            gifts, and we aren't able to use them in the context of
            the Church.

Korby   What I hear you saying is that the Church isn't doing
            much about it, and society isn't doing much about it.
            But if women themselves can band together and,
            say, have seminars and studies. . . .

Woman   Women have been having seminars for a long time,
            and have been banding together. What we've been
            saying in a way is that the Church as I perceive it at
            this point is a very unjust structure. And women are
            leaving this bad structure and continuing to live
            their Christian lives, and continuing to pray. But the
            Church is unable, inflexible, to meet them where
            they are in their journey. So they go to other
            churches to lead active Christian lives. So it's not
            that we need more groups. We need a change in the
            structure.

Korby   So then would it be fair to say that women's groups have to study, somehow, what they could do to facilitate a change in the structure.

Woman   I don't know that the women's groups have to do anything. I think that the structure needs to do something. I don't see that women need to do more. I don't think that the burden of proof here is on the women.

Korby   No, no, no. I don't mean that!

Woman   No. I don't mean to sound defensive. It's just that as a woman who is involved with other women, I know what women are doing. I am also involved with the Church and I know what the Church is not doing. And it just seems to me that the Church is becoming more and more entrenched. In trying to live up to the fullness of our gifts and the graces that we have received, more women are finding out that doesn't necessarily mean you do it within the context of the institution of the Church.

UGANDA

Korby   Do you think there are some people who are stepping out of the Catholic Church into other Christian churches because they see in other Christian churches more opportunity to develop their own potential as women?

Woman   Yes! Yes! Particularly over this issue of ordination.

Korby   Yeah.

Woman   I have known at least two women who have gone out of the Catholic Church because they want to be priests. They have become Anglicans in order to become priests.

Korby   Uh-huh.

Woman   So it is happening, and we hope the Catholic Church will not just stand by and let the women go . . . go out of the Church in order to find fulfillment.

Women's Organizations in the Church

Many women long for a forum in which they can speak their ideas freely. They also want women's study and social activism groups. It is important to teach other women to be conscious of their own dignity.

KENYA

Korby   What would you want from the Church, ideally, knowing that you are not going to have a lot of changes quickly?

Woman   I would ask that you see we only have the CWA, Catholic Women's Association, which doesn't seem to have done very much all these years. You see, we live under a shadow of these men. Whatever we do has to conform to what they say; we cannot say about this and that and that. But I think if women could be allowed to have a women's group, one that is really run by women, all women, and if we could be free to express the things that we are feeling, even if these are outlandish. Just like we are free here today.

Korby   These ideas aren't outlandish.

Woman   You are right, but these ideas are outlandish in any other forum. If we do have a forum for women, there are many stipulations. You shall not touch this subject, no, no. Let those women say what they want to say. And let them not be penalized for it, you, to be banned.

Korby   Banned and burned.

Woman   Yeah. In fact, many like this professor that I mentioned earlier aren't in the CWA, but I thought she should be, a person like her. There are many like her, talented and resourceful. But they wouldn't dare step foot into CWA because I think they cannot say some things. You know, this is a movement of the women. And the person at the top to tell you what to do is a man. And a man does not understand.

Korby   Uh-huh.

Woman   OK, there are women's groups. But those groups are not really involved in awakening in women their own dignity as persons, to begin to live life differently. It's more to try to alleviate, you know, the human problems like poverty, so that they can economically be able to support themselves, help them to be able to be economically self-sufficient.

        But I think, you know, they need to realize what causes their problems, rather than let me kind of get rid of this problem without knowing what the cause is. Because tomorrow that problem is going to emerge again. So unless we get to the roots of the problems, and the roots of the problems is the use and abuse, of seeing women as properties, as objects. And they are poor. Most of the poor people in this country are women. And these people are seen as objects of exploitation and use.

Korby   Yes. Are there many women who, let's say, who think as you do? They maybe don't express it in the same way, but they have the same ideas, the same principles you have?

Woman   Yes. The thing is, many are so afraid, so caught up in fear that they are not really able to break loose from the fear that they are not able to speak. In fact, when I am just with them we can speak and speak. But when we go in another kind of context they won't speak.

SOUTH AFRICA

Woman 1   We are just a group (of women). Sometimes we get together and pray for the sick people. And sometimes we sit outside and read the Bible, but we don't know how to do this. We want to, but we don't know how to.

Korby   OK. What you would like to do, I think what you are saying is you would like to have somebody to be able to lead you in a Bible study group, so that maybe you could get together once every two weeks for a couple of hours, with maybe one priest or a brother, or somebody, and just study what is in the Bible. What they are doing in many places in South America and Kenya and Uganda, I know for sure, is that they have base communities, people who get together and they just try to see how the Bible answers some of their problems.

Woman 1   But also we want, when we are out, the people are old and poor and we want to give them something, maybe clothes and food.

Woman 2   We can get materials and work together.

Korby   Probably what you will have to do is to try to convince women that they will be helping themselves by coming. It won't happen overnight. You ladies have a lot of patience, that I know. You have a lot of ability. You have so much intelligence, but you don't have the opportunity to use it.

Woman 2   We also live far away. It takes a whole day. We can say, "This day we are coming, that day."

Woman 3   We all here, we are not educated. That's why we have problems.

Korby   That's what I've heard. That's what women all over Africa say. "We need more education. We need people to come and lead seminars. We need workshops. We need people to come and show us how. We want to, but we don't know how."

SRI LANKA

Woman   I have thought up a strategy that we shouldn't talk of, uh, feminism like that. But you get it done the other way. See, somebody I know, some people returned recently after a seminar. And the Indian lady who was in charge of the women's desk had been talking so much feminism that all the men there got really angry.

Korby   Were turned off.

Woman   Yeah. So you shouldn't do that. Then you are losing more than gaining. So you should know how to handle it, but still you keep your dignity and achieve your dignity, I would say.

Korby   Yeah.

Woman   But we are building the grassroots. Whether you like it or not, it will come. Still again, I would repeat to you to tell these women of the West not to push that feminism. I have seen in Asian countries, there's a tendency for the men to throw you away.

Korby   So what you would say is, "Lay off the feminism and just work toward getting women more educated and aware."

Woman   Conscious of their own dignity.

NEW GUINEA

Korby   Is there a group of Catholic women in New Guinea?

Woman   We have our Federation for Catholic women and youth, Catholic teachers, Catholic nurses. One of our biggest problems is just that we need spiritual directors. A lot of us are taking up positions and don't know, really, what are the roles and functions.

 Now five years ago we had what they call a Catholic laity. The priests and officials were so frightened of this so-called association. They discouraged very much. And now it's come back to zero, disintegrated.

Korby   Um hum. Does it work best with groups of women like that to have a woman who is a leadership coordinator? Or does it work best if it's a man?

Woman   A woman.

Korby   A woman, yeah.

Woman   Let a woman do a woman's thing. Let the men do the men's problem.

Korby   OK. But most of the time it is more likely that there is a man as head, huh?

Woman   Yes.

Korby   And you would like to see it be a woman?

Woman   Yes, a woman would be better.

❖   ❖   ❖

NEW GUINEA

Woman 1   Are there any women's organizations in hiding?

Woman 2   The gardens, every Tuesday.

Woman 1   If there is an organization, tell them to come out of hiding. A letter to the editor or something.

❖   ❖   ❖

Narrative Three
The Power and the Right

NEW GUINEA

Woman   We can all tell stories. And I have my story, and I drag it in every time we talk about this. Back home I lived in a certain town which shall remain anonymous. I was the religious education coordinator for a school of nearly one-thousand students in a high school. It wasn't what you would call a position, but anyway that was the job. And, um, I had special training to do that job. And during that training I got a bachelors degree in theology, and I was pretty well equipped to do this job. But that's another story.

But anyway, I'm organizing the end-of-the-year graduation down at the parish church, and it's a big mess. And the parish priest was delighted to have this school, and is all big gung-ho pride. And we're having this graduation Mass. And for communion ministers of the graduation Mass, I'd asked the principal of the school, a Brother, if he would be one. And I said, "I'll be the other one." I mean, I'm the religious ed coordinator. It seemed appropriate that we'd be it. So we lined it all up.

Five minutes before the Mass started, here comes the priest: "Who's going to be the Communion ministers?"

And I said, "Brother and me." And he said, "You can't give out Communion."

And I said, "Uh, why not?"

And he said, "You haven't done the course." In this parish he had a course of two tape recordings that a priest friend of his had made. I don't know what was on them. Anyway, I hadn't listened to the two tapes. And I said, "Oh that's all right, Father, OK." I mean I wasn't going to cause a fuss this day of the graduation. We'd go to somebody else who had listened to the tapes.

But that's what I'm wondering about. If it had nothing to do with me listening to the tapes or not. It had a lot to do with his power.

And I mean we're talking about a priest who is a very highly educated man. I mean, you know, real thoughtful. But he'd never been encouraged to look at his own actions in society. I mean, we ended up, I said, "Look, you've got the power to stop me, mate, but you haven't got the right." We left it at that. But it was about something else. It wasn't about listening to the tape.

Chapter Four

The Hierarchical Church

Seminary Education

Change must occur in the seminaries at which priests are trained. Bring more women onto seminary faculties, and treat them as equals. Allow women to study theology alongside the men training for priesthood.

KENYA

Korby   I suppose the priests are just going along with the culture again. And their seminary training has not turned that around. So I guess we've got to get busy and do something in the seminaries, don't we?

Woman   That's where we have to go. But you see, they don't have women teaching in those seminaries. OK, and when they wanted women to teach in that seminary, they don't treat you as a professional.

Korby   We had that problem at the seminary where I taught.

Woman   One of the seminaries in Kenya asked me to teach for them. I taught for them for a semester. But I was not treated as a professional. And actually, I was going to teach because they wanted me to continue teaching for them. And it was painful for me to say no. But I had to because I said I was not going to be used and abused. I am a professional and I should be treated that way.

Korby   Absolutely. At the same time, of course, the students did not benefit from what you would have been able to give them. But your own survival comes first.

Woman   You are right. So I felt, you know, like OK, women are there. But they are not willing to take these women as professionals so they can bring the feminist perspective to the teaching of theology in the seminary. And it has to be, in order to have a balanced formation for the priests.

Korby   Right, so that the priests who come out will be aware and keep working at it.

Woman   Yeah. Because I don't think there is any of that awareness at all. In our national seminary, women are not there. They don't even invite them.

SRI LANKA

Woman   I have taught thirty years in the private school. Now I am teaching in the seminary.

Korby   Good for you! How are you accepted by the priests on the faculty there? Do they treat you as equal with them?

Woman   There are no difficulties.

Korby   Good. Are there lay people on the faculty also?

Woman   Yes.

Korby   Yes, good. And they treat you equal. That's wonderful! Because in some places it doesn't work that way.

NEW GUINEA

Korby   It looks to me, from what you have been saying here, that the point that has to be stressed to the furthest extent possible is the training of the present priests, the training of the priests who are going to be ordained in the future.

Woman   Right, Father's right.

Korby   So that they will be really pastoral priests and be open to these kinds of things and move with it.

Woman   Yes.

Korby   So then the question comes back, how do we get that into the seminary? You'll have to start coming up here and teach these kids!

Woman   It'll probably be a scandal if the three of us (women) were to come and sit there and talk about the Church's policy toward women. It would be a scandal for them if a nun — Oh God! — would come in and sit down and give them a talk. There's a difference. And maybe, why are they are afraid of us? Are we sex objects, or what?

Korby   I don't know.

Woman   I don't know. But something has to break through in the seminary to include the influence of women. And I think women should also be encouraged to come to seminary. . . .

Korby   . . . to . . .

Woman   . . . study scripture. I was working up here once, and
               I really wanted to do theology. Just to have a deeper
               understanding of the faith. That's all we need. But
               the seminary doesn't open itself to laity.

Korby   Yeah, that's where we were really lucky at the semi-
               nary where I was teaching. We had a man there who
               was the head of the seminary who was open-
               minded. So we had a couple of lay married women
               who went through and took all of the studies. And
               now, one of those women is an assistant academic
               dean, she's a spiritual director for the students there,
               and she's just doing a magnificent job. It brings the
               whole feminine perspective in there.

Woman   Yeah. Maybe some motherly touch.

NEW GUINEA (ANOTHER SEMINARY)

Woman   I worry about what ideas are passed on to the men in
               the seminary. I think it's much better here now than
               it was before. Ten years ago, you would not have
               found women welcome in this seminary to teach.

Korby   Really? So it's changed pretty fast.

Woman   She [another woman present] is on the staff full-
               time, and I'm on the staff part-time. And I've heard
               two of the national priests say to me "It's nice to have
               another woman on the staff." It shows the growth in
               them.
                   But I think in the seminary is where [future priests]
               have to be made to appreciate. I try to do it as much
               as I can. I mean, I'm not, you know, a radical femi-

nist. I believe maybe "inclusive-ness" is a better word than a "feminist." I don't know if "inclusiveness" is a word, even. But maybe we'll create it.

Korby   Right. But too many times what happens is that while they're in the seminary they'll be accepting these ideas, and they're open and so forth. But once they get back out on their own, back out with the older clergy again, they revert back to their old ideas. So in a sense it's kind of a veneer which gets put on and gets peeled off afterwards.

Woman   Oh, I think that that's what happens here, too. But ...

Korby   But for some of them it sticks.

Lay Ministry

Lay leadership can give continuity to a church community. It is one area in which women have made great strides toward equality. Yet in some localities, lay leadership in the Church is still resisted by clergy.

SRI LANKA

Woman   I feel that the Church has all these associations, but it doesn't go to the people, it doesn't touch their problems. It doesn't touch the hearts of the people. It doesn't touch their lives. We've spoken about this, training leaders and giving opportunity to the lay. But the priests are afraid. They don't support it enough.

Korby   I heard somebody say, "What we need is people who have the courage in Christ to go against the culture." Not to be defensive about this, but to break through some of this stuff. What I think you are saying here is that the activity has to be primarily in the parish. You have to have a priest who is open-minded, and give the laity an opportunity to work. You need a trained lay leader. You need somebody who will be supportive of all the groups you've mentioned, a leader who can constantly make the people and priests, everybody, aware of the fact that we need to work more for equality. A lay leader who is strong enough and courageous enough to challenge even the priests. Right? Give them a little . . . push.

Woman   The priests are transferred. So each priest has his own mission, own interest. The sisters are moved, too. Therefore, it's truly the laity who must be leading. They should tell the priests, "This is what we are doing."

Korby   Yeah, the lay leaders are not transferred.

Woman   They won't leave the village. They are always here.

Korby   After all, it's the people who are the Church, really. You know, the Holy Spirit inspiring them with courage and hope and so on.

NEW GUINEA

Woman 1   A lot of us are frustrated because we are under-utilized. A lot of us lay people, we can give to the Church on our own time. And some of us are doing that already. But thousands of people that we know haven't been approached to assist. A perfect example, the seminary we are sitting in here. How many lay people like us would come to the seminary and be welcomed; be welcomed into the library to do some studies? To be welcomed into their workshops to sit and listen to what they say? To what scripture is being newly interpreted for us? It's just for you. None of us come here for that kind of thing. Our faith has been given to us and let die. A friend is supposed to be growing.

Woman 2   Well, in parishes here we have what we call parish council. And within the parish councils we have different committees for different things. But those committees only exist within the parishes. And how would those committees work if there is nobody coming in and helping, encouraging them, and teaching them what they should be teaching?

Korby   Are there seminars or workshops to help to train them?

Woman 1   Only when you request them. And in parishes where people don't know about this type of thing, they do not ask for it.

Woman 2   You know, Father, they don't seem to use the lay apostolate like Vatican II asks for. The utilization of lay people. Is it that they are afraid of diluting their power? Or losing the priesthood because they are giving more authority to other people?

Korby   So your hands really are tied. You can't develop the gifts that you have.

Woman 2   No. That's right.

Woman 1   We are very powerful women in the government. Come to the Catholic Church, forget it.

Korby   I'm just wondering whether something more might be done if the lay people just would really go ahead on their own, without the leadership of the priests. Have some people come in to present seminars and workshops on how to lead, and what to do, and all that.

Woman   OK, I'll give an example. Last Sunday we had a meeting for the Friends of the Library for the seminary. Now we were approached by Father to assist in the seminary. And we thought this is part of our contribution to the Church. Our participation and our assistance. Laity forming themselves into an association to assist the Library of the Seminary. OK, we came on Sunday and had a meeting. And we had at the back of our ears that we have local priests who don't agree with this kind of thing. Concrete example, right here.

Korby   Exactly.

Woman   We were supposed to have a barbecue. The seminarians who were supposed to be in charge of the library prepared a barbecue. And we were supposed to come with our families, bring food. And afterwards, the meeting was to finalize the Constitution of the association. We'd been meeting the whole year, you see. And we'd been fundraising. And then we were told that some priests have decided that we would not have a barbecue. So we caught on. This is just an example I'm citing to you. It's a very concrete example, one which happens all the time.

Korby   So you didn't have your barbecue then?

Woman   No. Do you know what we did? We forget the seminary priests, all our local priests here. We went straight to the bishop. I don't know what is the outcome. I'm still waiting.

Korby Well, I know! We had a meeting yesterday with the bishop. He approved it! So it looks to me like you do have success by going around — in football we say an end run. And go right to the top like you did to the bishop.

Woman Well, that's OK. But that should not happen. We should be respected.

Korby No, but if that's the only . . .

Woman What I'm saying is, then, we must be recognized and respected in our own capacity.

Korby But to get there in the first place, you know, it must be . . .

Woman Initially.

Korby The initial way of doing it. Not as a general way of doing it, but in order to break through the impasse which seems to be here.

Woman I mean the structure of the Church is very men-dominated anyway.

Fr. Dave You've got to get their attention. I remember a story about this man. A farmer bought a mule from another farmer. So the guy who bought the mule couldn't make him work so he goes back to the other man and said, "What kind of mule did you sell me? He won't do anything."

The farmer said, "Oh, he will too. I'll come and show you." So they went back. "Where's the mule?"

"Over here."

"OK, hook him up." So the owner that sold him took a 2 x 4 and knocked him to the ground.
He says, "First you've got to get his attention!"

Woman 1   Maybe this is what probably we need to do!

Woman 2   That's what we need to do, yeah. Get their attention by marching up to the Bishops Conference and say (slap) this is what we want! Bang, bang, bang, bang.

Korby   With all the reasons why it would be better for the bishops in the Church to do it that way, rather than the way it's being done now. You'd have to spell out the reasons.

Fr. Dave   I'm glad I'm leaving today. I see a hornet's nest brewing here!

SRI LANKA

Woman   We conduct weekends for men and women. It is an experience with giving the essence of Christianity in a very concise form. We take them out for three days. Of course, men separated, women separated. For the men we have a team of lay men who conduct all the lectures and the talks, and women for the women. It is one place where I have experienced equality among men and women.

Korby   You mentioned that men give the lectures for men, and women for the women.

Woman   That is only for the initiation, to begin with. After that, we work together.

Korby   Is there a follow-up?

Woman   Yes. We ask each of these members who have participated in this weekend to meet weekly in groups of three and share your life of piety, study, and action.

Korby   Do the men listen?

Woman   They do. But it depends on what area we're working. You know, we have different areas. Liturgy, education, development, we have different divisions. So now, of course, if you take the liturgy, most of us in it are ladies. There are some men in that as well, but in that area there isn't much difference. We work together, each one listens to the other, and we really take a leading role there. Maybe we plan a liturgy for each Sunday.

    Then, of course, when it comes to human development, in those areas you will find mostly the men. I don't know whether they are purposely kept apart, whether it is due to discrimination, or whether they feel that men are in a better position to go out and work. But I suppose they could give us a try!

Korby   Experiment, huh?!

Woman   Their meetings are late at night. The women here are still not liberated in that sense. They can't get into a car and drive around. That's a big limiting factor. Getting somebody to take them home.

Woman 2   It's a big drawback, Father.

Korby   Is it just simply dangerous to be out late at night? Is that the reason? Or is it that they, it's not the thing to do?

Woman   Culturally.

❖   ❖   ❖

NEW GUINEA

Korby   What are things that ought to be worked on right now that are not being done? Anything come to mind?

Woman   Just generally on the parish level, more involvement of women in what's going on in the parish. Not just to sit at a meeting and not say anything, and let the men do all the talking. You know? Sometimes you have to get the women by themselves and say, "What do you think?"

Korby   Yeah.

Woman   And making things available for them to do, like the women's conference. That's backed by the bishops. So that's why it's moving. It's sad to say, but in a way it's good. The bishops are beginning to realize that women have something to contribute.

Fr. Dave A very rich resource that has not been investigated or tapped. I was talking to a priest last night at the cocktail party. And I described to him my idea about the Holy Spirit working in our country, the lack of both priests and vocations. I think it's giving a very clear message. There's all kinds of talent among the lay people. The Spirit working through them, you know.

Woman   That's my argument. It's about time we recognized the beauty of the laity.

Hierarchy and the Feminine Side of God

Korby hears that for many women, equality is not simply a matter of being "let in" to participate in the decision-making process, or being invited into ordained hierarchy. The problem, for these women, is the hierarchy itself. A structure that places power in the hands of a few blinds itself to the feminine aspects of God and lessens the Church's ability to empathize with the problems of people. To merely *join* such a hierarchy would solve no problems. These women hope that the Holy Spirit will be able to "break through" and re-create a less hierarchical Church.

ENGLAND

Woman 1   I was going to say, Father, that the equality of women in the Church is going to have to change anyway because the secular world has overtaken us and passed us out, by miles, really.

Korby   Would anybody here have any idea of why it is that things have gotten worse in the Church than in the secular world?

Woman 2   Because of the men, I think, at the top. I mean it's very, I find it very disheartening in Rome to go and see the whole college of cardinals, all the bishops, and all the priests. And some people think it's a marvelous spectacle and a wonderful dressing up with their miters and their coats and their paraphernalia. I find it dreadfully pompous and auspicious. A show of power. Now underneath they can be very simple men. But we — the laity — expect them to dress up in this. And I think if women were within this sector of the Church there would be a simplicity of style. I feel quite strongly about that.

KENYA

Woman   I think that it's very difficult to have equality in a hierarchical structure. To be in a society where decisions are made for you, where your experience and your input is not valued and is disregarded . . .

Korby   It's not Christian, is it?

Woman   It isn't, no. It's not very human either! Let alone being Christian. So rather than saying, you know, women should be ordained or this or that, there are certain givens that have to be in place before anything else can happen. People should be valued because of their contributions irrespective of their color or their size or their gender.

ENGLAND

Woman   It's important, isn't it, Father, that while we look at God we see the feminine aspects of God just the same as we see the feminine and masculine aspects in each of ourselves. And I think that that is coming out of a lot of the New Age thinking, that this Mother God is coming back again. Now perhaps that will fill our psychological needs there.

NEW GUINEA

Woman   The core of it is the power issue. If you challenge or even question, dare to question anything at an official level, you very soon get labeled and put in your box. Now I would have to qualify that by saying individually I have worked with a lot of priests and bishops who have been helpful. Individually these Church members in the hierarchical structure are fine people. And they will sit down and they will talk person-to-person, and listen to what you've got to say. But let them come together at a meeting or a Bishops' conference, and, well, you may as well not exist. So in that I find a great contradiction, and it must be a struggle within themselves. Because they are victims of the system, too.

Korby   Uh huh.

Woman   I think the clergy as we know it is dying, will finish very soon. New forms of ministry, new forms of priesthood are emerging. And certainly by the turn of the century, the current crop of clergy will be left behind. People are indifferent. They are forming other forms of worshipping communities.

WEST SENECA, NEW YORK

Woman   I took a couple of courses in liberation theology, and one of the big things I understood is that theology is not separate from life. Theology comes from the lived experience.

Korby   Right.

Woman   And that's one reason why the theology coming out of South America is so progressive, and there is so much of it, because the Church is so alive, and saying so much, and these people are taking this and putting it into books, and I think you need to help people realize that they are the theologians. The Pope is not the primary theologian.

Korby   To put it another way, a theologian has to be a person with a daily newspaper in one hand, and a Bible in the other, and then you put the two together.

UGANDA

Woman   If the Church can just let go and let the Holy Spirit be the guide because right now the Holy Spirit has been controlled so long. I think for the last two thousand years the Holy Spirit has been controlled. Occasionally, the Spirit breaks through and is controlled again, breaks through and is controlled again. I thought Vatican II had broken through, but it's being controlled again.

Korby   Uh huh. Everything is being thrown back. Whatever was going in this direction is now being turned back and tied up again.

Woman   It is!

Korby   I've heard some women say that they've just given up on the structure, that the structure within the Church is such that it can't be "cracked," that it won't be "cracked," that the Holy Spirit is not going to be able to do it. We have to change the structure.

Woman   Yes, I think that the structure itself has to go. That's part of my personal opinion. And when the structure goes, you know, then we will see that the Spirit is not just in one man, but the Spirit is in all individuals in the Church. And the Spirit is coming forth, and drawing the Church together by inspiring all these other people. And until we come to that, I think the structure is yet going to continue lording it over, and telling us that this is what the Spirit is.

Korby   What would . . . the structure has to go in what sense?

Woman   For me, this hierarchical model . . . (pauses)

Korby   It's OK. I won't say who said it. I'll just say that there are certain women in Africa who are thinking this, and let's not say that they aren't, you know?

Woman   In this hierarchical model it is believed that the higher you are in that model, the closer you are to God and the Holy Spirit talks to the person who is on top more than the person who is on the bottom. I don't believe it!

Korby   Unfortunately, there are people who think that way about priests. And that was not the idea of Vatican II.

Woman   Even if you put the Pope at the center, still it is going in circles, and the last ring is going to be the outside.

Korby   If it weren't for the Holy Spirit, you'd think the situation were hopeless, huh?

Woman   So for me, I think that we should not put the Pope at the center, the Pope should be in one of the rings. That is my kind of structure.

Korby   Uh huh.

Woman   I think that each Church in each country should have its own leadership; they are the ones who know what their problems are. And Rome should really aim at listening. Rome should not be dictating to Kenya what should be done, huh? Or to the United States what should be done. They should be listening to the United States, and they should be listening to Kenya and saying, "What can we learn from the situation and conditions of the Christians, the Catholics from that place?" Rather than, you know, imposing their own views and opinions.

Korby   I was thinking of something else. I was thinking of Rome, or the Pope, not being in a position of imposing, but being kind of a facilitator. Cross-facilitating ideas and so forth. And saying, "Well, have you thought about this?" You know? "Well, think about it. If it's helpful, OK, and if it's not, that's all right, too."

New Guinea

Woman   I was in Germany two weeks ago. And at the seminar, a lot of people were talking about God as a woman. God as a mother. And, well, I never really looked at God that way. We were always told that God is always a man, OK?

Kenya

Woman   You say that we are created in the image of God. I say I look like God, is it? Now when Luke and Mark write the Bible, they always talk about God and man. And remember we are equal. So who decided this?

Korby   Who decided what?

Woman   That God should be a man.

Korby   That's the culture.

Woman   Yeah, it's the culture. It's always the men will say that God is a man. See how it is, the Bible, how it is written.

Korby   The "image and likeness of God," as I have understood it from the scripture scholars, the men who really get into studying the scripture in the context of the culture in which it was written, say this "image and likeness" means that each individual has intellect and will. That they can think, and that they can love, and that they are created to live in community. The equality as I would see it would be that God has given each one — God, he/she, she/he — has given each one intellect and will and the ability to live in community. And he wants each of us to be able to exercise her full potential, or his full potential. And that is where equality comes, in being given the opportunity to live one's gifts that God has given.

Narrative Four

The Veil

Korby You, in a sense, being a sister, are more free to speak. Right? Because you don't have to kowtow to a husband or somebody like that.

Woman Actually, there was one time I got in trouble for speaking out. A journalist came to me and said, "Sister, I would like to have a story from you for the newspaper." And I said, "What story do you want from me?" She said, "Any of your feminist papers or anything you want to give me." So I gave her a paper I had written on the condition of women in ____. Now she took this paper, and I said, "Now just look through it and you can pick up whatever you want to."

Meanwhile, she started asking me questions. And me, I didn't even know that these questions were going to be in the article. I thought that the article was going to be about the paper I gave her. So she asked me, "Sister, what do you think of the veil?"

And I said, "Oh, a veil? It has really no meaning for me. But I wear it because of the conditions in our Church here. I have to wear it in order to remain a sister because if I didn't wear it, I would be told to quit. And I still want to be a sister." And I said, "You know, it is a form of oppression. Why do the bishops [of this country] demand that sisters wear veils, wear habits, wherever they are, even in their own houses, and they don't demand that from their priests?"

I told her the sisters are the maids of the Church. You know, like in the household you have maid servants. Most of the households here have servants. So I said, "In the Church, the household servants are the sisters. So they are the handmaids for the Church."

So this goes complete in the papers. Oh my God! The phone calls I received, the letters I got, the summons I got. It was like three months of nightmare. X said I should write a letter to the editor and withdraw what I said. And in my conscience I didn't think of doing that.

Korby   That would be another kind of oppression.

Woman   So now I say, what do I do? This is now a matter of obedience. So I had to write the letter because now it was either my religious life or this letter.

The Cardinal came, actually came here in person, to see me. And he said, "My child, what is it? What is going wrong?" But he was so understanding. I told him, "Cardinal, I was so shocked, just as you were shocked, because I never expected that in the paper."

And he said, "Yes, I knew that because you always wear your veil!" Finally he said, "OK, don't worry about it, and don't write anything to the newspaper. Don't write. Just leave it like that. If anybody writes to the paper, let them write. But you don't get involved. Just leave it."

And there were some people who called me and they said thank you for your courage.

Chapter Five

Korby's Voice

WEST SENECA, NEW YORK

Korby   I came to realize what the Church is missing when I was working very, very closely with a woman on the faculty at the Josephinum. Ladora had been a Dominican nun for a few years and left the order in all good graces, got a degree in religious education, and generally the administration heard about her as being a really fine person, and hired her to help me out with directing the pastoral care training of the seminarians. After a while she was really directing the pastoral training, and I began to see that we had to really relate to each other. I haven't ever been married, but I think we had to relate as closely as husband and wife in order for me to know what she was thinking, and for her to know what I was thinking. And I knew when her bad days were, and all the rest of it. And I began to just kind of feel for her the hurt she experienced from the way she was treated by some of the men on the faculty, particularly by priests who came to the U.S. from Europe.

And I just made my mind up that if I lived as far as my retirement and had the time to do it, I was going to do something to try to bring about an alleviation of this.

And at the same time I could see the way she looked at things, in the training of the guys that were going to be priests, was not a way in which I looked at it a lot of times. I mean, there was more sensitivity for the nourishment of life. Sensitive to the needs, to how decisions were going to affect people's feelings.

UGANDA

Korby   That's what I was maintaining, that some of the people in Rome were saying that it is only in the U.S. and Canada and a couple of European countries where women are really interested in having real equality and acceptance of dignity and respect, etc., and wanting to really have the opportunity to develop themselves, and that they are radical feminists. And I said, "I don't believe it; they're in other countries of the world. I think they're all through the Third World. And so that's what we're doing. Just going to see what it is that you're saying. I'm trying to do this as a kind of qualitative research rather than quantitative.
. . . I'd like to hear from the ladies and the men both, but especially from the ladies. I'd like to hear the ladies say what they think regardless of what they think their husbands think. And then we'll give you absolution afterwards!

INDIA

Korby   There was a lady up in Fairbanks, Alaska, who pointed something out to me. She's a lay person who was directing the liturgy for the whole diocese. And she pointed out to me that in a letter from St. Paul to the Ephesians, he says that in Christ all are one.

There is neither male nor female, neither Jew nor Gentile, neither slave nor free. . . . Everybody is . . .

Woman Is equal.

Korby Is equal, right. And that that little phraseology was, one scripture scholar has said, part of an early Christian Creed. That it really was something that people would recite like we do the Apostle's Creed. That they really believed in this equality. And that that had come from Christ. That was the way they saw what Jesus taught.

   (Same discussion, from Kenya) Now St. Paul was able to do something about treating the Jews and the Gentiles the same to get into the Church. But slave and free, he couldn't do anything about because he would have upset the whole world in trying to do it. And so it, you know, like in the United States, it's only been back in the 1800's, a hundred and thirty years ago that we got rid of slavery. So it's a growth, I think, in understanding and movement toward equality.

   But there were a lot of other things that happened. And so from the Jewish culture and the Latin culture and the Greek culture, and the men who were writing the New Testament, all that equality that Jesus was trying to tell people, that kind of got washed away. And that's why the scripture scholars have to go back and sort of de-culturalize the message of scripture.

KENYA

Korby I had just said something about how I'd decided fifteen years ago that if the Lord gave me energy to do such and such, and a woman who is on the faculty at the seminary said to me, "Father, if you don't mind, I would just like to mention something to you. I belong to a group of minorities, but I believe that we ought to have inclusive language. I don't see any way in which you can speak about God as Lord and not be speaking about God in the sense of being male. Because a Lord is a man, see?" And I said, "By golly, you're right! Thanks for telling me." In spite of my really wanting to do my best, there was a mistake that I was making. And then I tried that night praying my breviary, and every time the word "Lord" came up, I put in "Yahweh" instead. My Lord, I bet it was three hundred times!

INDIA

Fr. Dave Jesus himself went against human traditions when he was living. He talked to the woman at the well and the disciples came back, "Well, what are you doing with her?" Here was a Jew talking to a Samaritan woman. He didn't worry about those human traditions.

Korby No. And the same with the Pharisees. He was telling them, you know, that they were manufacturing all kinds of human traditions and making the people follow them, and they were forgetting the essence of the thing. And I wonder, that's what we need to study, then, to find out what really is human tradition, and what is divine tradition.

 And there have been studies made. Karl Rahner, I know, had one of his students make a special study about whether there is anything in theology or in the definitions of the Church which said that women could not be ordained. And the conclusion that they came to was "no." There's nothing there.

So it looks from studies like this that it is just simply human tradition. Maybe part of the problem that is in the Church is that it doesn't want to go against the human tradition and turn people upside down without having people educated enough. But then what we have to do is get them educated. And it seems like more might be able to be done that way.

I was talking with some sisters in Bombay the other day, and one of the things that came up there was that maybe what we can do is have more women theologians, sisters who become theologians and teach, and then they can teach in the seminaries, maybe some time in the future. Then they will be able to educate the priests more, so that the priests will be more open and more aware and understand what the women are suffering, and do something to change it.

I was not always this way. I have always liked women, I like to be with them, in their company and so on. But I never realized what pain women were going through because of the inequities that were there until I was working together with a lady and I began to realize the pain that she was suffering because of the way she was being treated by other priests on our faculty. And that's when I made up my mind, by golly, I'm going to try and do something if at all possible. So I had to experience it in some way in order to wake up to it.

INDIA

Korby   Of course right now the ordination of women is against the legislation of the Church. But in studies of theology by Karl Rahner and by a bishop in the

United States they have come to the conclusion that there is nothing in theology and there is nothing in scripture which is against the idea of ordination. Rather that Jesus did not call any women to be apostles like the men because, culturally speaking, they just would not have been listened to. They would not have been heard. But that Jesus really did treat women very equally. He broke through all kinds of taboos that were in the Jewish society. He wasn't supposed to touch women, he wasn't supposed to talk with them, he wasn't supposed to really communicate with them, and he did all the way through. You know, with Mary Magdalene, with Martha, there were a group of women who were helping him all the time. I remember one writer putting it that it is really a sign of his divinity that he treated Mary Magdalene the way he did, and the woman who was caught in adultery, and the woman who came up and touched the hem of his cloth, you know. So that the Christian message really was that men and women should be equal in dignity, equal in respect, all the way through.

So at the present time it's really just a traditional position that women cannot be ordained.

So maybe that's one thing that can be done is if the women around the world keep asking the question, "Why can't we be ordained?" And still keep asking, asking, asking, asking, and praying. You know? Yeah, just like it says in the Gospel, somebody comes to the door and the guy's in bed and he doesn't answer. Finally he answers because he is tired of just being pestered.

INDIA

Korby   I was one place where the priests can't get there for six months at a time, and so the sisters take care of everything in the parish. Of course, she can't have Mass, but she talks with the people, she counsels them, and so forth. And they tell her everything that they would tell a priest if they were going to confession, but she can't give them absolution. She is able to give them Communion. The bishop said, "You go ahead and give them Communion. You have everything except the Consecration." Some of the people even think it's Mass, but it's not, you know. When the bishop came there, the people just flocked around him and said what a good job Sister was doing of taking care of the parish and offering Mass. They just misunderstood. It didn't bother them at all.

See, sometimes they say that we can't ordain women as priests because the people wouldn't want that. Well, here was this whole parish who thought that she was having Mass, and it didn't make a difference at all!

NEW GUINEA

Korby   I do think that people, instead of leaving the Catholic Church, should prod their priests and those in the Church to "Hey, open for us the gifts!" Somebody said last night, "The Church is ailing, but the Church is your mother. Do you leave your mother when she's sick?"

KENYA

Woman   I wanted to ask you a question. Aren't you afraid that all this — your research — will lead to you being derailed or even accused of promoting people out of the priesthood?

Korby   I've been swimming upstream for years, so I'm just not worried about it at all.

Woman   It doesn't worry you at all?

Korby   No. Well, in another sense, I am in a situation where I don't have to be worried about it. Because no matter what people in the Church would say about it, I could still keep on doing it. Although if I were living at the seminary where I taught — that's part of the retirement benefits which I declined — things could be different. But on my own I decided to move away from there. So that on the one hand I wouldn't embarrass them, and on the other hand I would be more free to express whatever I wanted without having somebody looking over my shoulder.

INDIA

Korby   I'll tell you what I think about equality. I think that Jesus said that he came so we could have life, and have it to the full. He came that you might have life and that you might have it abundantly. And that's for every man and woman to have full life. So what he would like to have is that everybody is able to develop all of their abilities, all of their potential so that they can really grow to their full stature. You know, like we have the trees out here. Well, you take a little seed and put it in the ground, and if you put it in the shade and put other trees over the top of it, and if you don't give it any water, it's not going to grow. But if you put it in the right place and you give it the kind of water that it needs, and give it some fertilizer, and give it sunshine, then it's really going to grow, and you get flowers and everything else. So that, I think Jesus is saying that he came so that we could be able to grow and become everything that he wanted us to be. Does that make sense?

Woman   Yeah.

Korby   Now, can you do that?